For skygrabbers everywhere

AND JIM, WITH FOREVER LOVE

touch the sky!

**FIND YOUR VOICE
SPEAK YOUR TRUTH
MAKE YOUR MARK**

Eleni Kelakos

Eleni Kelakos Enterprises, Ltd.

ISBN 978-0-9816882-1-3
eISBN 978-0-9816882-2-0

Library of Congress Control Number: 2012915042

Printed in the United States of America

The quotes from the songs "Touch the Sky," "Hope Begins with Me," "Choir," "Change," and "If I Were Me" are from the album *Touch the Sky* by Eleni Kelakos, ©Leg E Cat Music, 2008, and are reproduced by permission.

The quotes from the song "The Tallest Poppy" are from the album *To The Bone* by Eleni Kelakos, © Leg E Cat Music, 2001, and are reproduced by permission

The quotes from the song "I Will Fly" are from the album *I Will Fly* by Eleni Kelakos, © Leg E Cat Music, 1999, and are reproduced by permission.

The quotes from the song "Into the Wild Why Not" are by Greg Greenway, © Sheen of Heat Music, 1998, and are reproduced by permission.

Book Design and Layout by Somberg Design /www.sombergdesign.com
Photography by Pierre Gautreau

Table of Contents

Foreword

Rare indeed, you are.

In your hands you hold what could possibly be the keys to your future.

You would not be reading this unless you had a burning desire to dig a little deeper within yourself and close the gap between what you are currently doing and what you want to achieve.

Once in a blue moon a person comes along who can change the course of our life and work. Eleni is one of those special people. Maybe she has already had an impact in your life. If not, get ready: Her wisdom, her vulnerability, her truth, and her insights will inspire you to a new level of courage and authenticity.

Make her book your bedside or desktop companion. Refer to it often and let the timeless principles move you to action in a way that might have been missing.

Through this book, her teachings, coaching, workshops, and music, Eleni can help you—the real you—stand up, embrace your story, and share your gifts with the world. Allow Eleni into your heart and mind. Let her firmly move you in the direction of your dream.

Once you do, your life will never be the same.

Mark LeBlanc
Author of *Growing Your Business* and *Never Be the Same*

Overture

AGE SIX

"Go! Now!"
Our teacher's voice, hissing.
We tumble out of the darkness onto the wooden stage, a giggling gaggle of
kindergarten girls, swishing multi-colored crepe paper skirts.
Rrrrrrrrrrrrrrrrip!
I catch my foot on my paper skirt. A ragged hole!
But I don't care. It's all so exciting. It's all so new.
My heart is pounding in a good, funny way.
People in seats, watching—Mummy is out there! I can feel her.
The piano plinks a melody. I know this song!
I open my mouth and bellow:
"She'll be coming 'round the mountain when she comes…"
I sing for Mummy. I sing because it feels so good. I sing to the seats in the back
row. My voice ricochets back at me.
We skip in time to the piano, skirts whirling.
I feel a hundred eyes watching, the seams of the stage underfoot.
The lights warm my face.
Applause wraps me like a big hug
I like this. I really like this.
No, I love this.

And so, it begins.

There is a song in you. The song of your soul.

Quiet, like a whisper. But there, always there. If you're willing to hear it. If you're willing to listen. If you're willing to pay attention.

Your very own song. A song that reflects your essential yumminess—your unique and special talents, abilities, dreams and desires, passion and purpose. The song in you sings you into being, into the moment, into the now. It's pulsing, insistent. It asks to be honored, cultivated, shared with the world, sung with arms flung wide open.

And when you do, when you actually do sing it and share it with all of your heart, you live in the richness and the fullness that is your birthright.

And when you don't? When you silence the song in you, make it small, step on it like a scurrying cockroach, slam a lid down—WHAM!—on the whispered strains of the song in you, life becomes less than it could be. Less full of color, commitment, clarity, purpose, joy—less full of you.

You are in the midst of your own perfect life. Is your life full of you? Are you choosing to honor the song in you? Are you choosing to touch the sky, to reach for the best in you? Are you choosing to sing and share the song in you? Or are you choosing to make yourself—and the song in you—your dreams, desires, talents, abilities—small?

If you're choosing to silence the song in you, well, hey, join the club: The world is filled with people who freeze, pause, shrink, and flee when faced with the opportunity and responsibility of embracing, nurturing, and sharing the song in them. Because it's easy to live a life unexamined, unconscious, and underdeveloped. It's easy to turn on the TV, overload yourself with meaningless tasks, worry about stuff you can't control, reach for the box of cookies, and pour another glass of Chardonnay. It's easy to stay away from the day-to-day, lifelong responsibility of singing the song in you, realizing, and sharing the best in you.

I know. Because that's what I did for far too long. I know what it's like to silence my voice, and keep myself small. I did it because I was scared. I did it because it was easier. I did it because I didn't know any better. I did what came naturally, the easier path.

But I eventually learned that easier is not necessarily better. I learned that the hard way.

And the hard way taught me there's nothing more wretched and sad than a soul-song unsung.

Putting it brutally and bluntly, close your eyes and imagine you, on the final day, in the final moments, of your life. Imagine that the song in you—your passion, your purpose, your unique dreams, desires, talents, and abilities—is unexplored and unshared. Your book is unwritten; the work with underprivileged children, undone; the paintings you swore you'd create, never attempted; your strong beliefs and opinions never shared. Is this what you want? I think not. I hope not.

This book exists to remind you that you matter, the song in you matters, and you are meant to embrace it, cultivate it, and sing it to the world, even—and especially—when challenges loom and you want to lock yourself in the basement with a gallon of chocolate Haagen Daz ice cream.

Throughout this book I use my personal story as a performing artist—along with stories and case studies culled from my work as a life coach, speech coach, and public speaking skills trainer—to illustrate my points. Chapters are ordered more by concept than chronology of events. At the end of each chapter, I turn the spotlight squarely on you: In a section called "Points to Ponder," I challenge you to explore the theme and lesson of the chapter, and its applications to your life and work. I end each chapter with "Say AAA," a series of questions and creative exercises designed to nudge you to examine your Attitude about the particular chapter theme, determine Actions you can take to move forward, and create a system of Accountability to help you take those actions.

Great actors, great presenters, and conscious, realized people honor the first commandment of great acting, speaking, and leading: "Know Thyself." Taking the time to figure out who you are, what you believe, what you know, what works for you, and what holds you back, is key to creating meaningful work and a fulfilling life that reflects your authentic essence.

You are not put on this earth to play small. You are here to realize the best in you and to touch the sky. The world is waiting for you, for exactly what you have to offer. Now is the only moment there is. So leap in and rise to your occasion. Your life awaits!

CHAPTER ONE

Your Passion and Purpose— Follow the Cosmic Clues

"The most powerful weapon on earth is the human soul on fire."
—FERDINAND FOCH[1]

I was born a diva, four pounds, fifteen ounces of screaming preemie. What I lacked in size, I made up for with a well-developed set of lungs and a relentless, colicky cry powerful enough to wake our neighbors. I insisted on being heard. At least in the beginning.

Yes, I was born a diva, prone to performing and drawn to the stage. But don't take my word for it: I have evidence. Hard, cold evidence in the form of a book called *Baby's Milestones—Birth to Seven Years*, a record of my development that my mom, Theresa, managed to keep until I basically wore her out by age three. Here's what Ma wrote about me under "Special Aptitudes":

"Loves to dance to music. Likes a tune, although bound to be loud and deep voiced. Has good rhythm and mimics well. Remembers songs and words well. Good Memory. Sizeable repertoire."

It also says, "Exercises in the sunlight, free of clothing." This is, I admit, still true.

Ma's written words are more than a description of my early aptitudes. They're big, fat clues —or, more specifically, cosmic clues, as I like to term them. Cosmic clues are clues that point you in the direction of what you're here to be and do while you're spending time on this planet. The cosmic clues reveal important aspects of the song in you, illuminating your passion and purpose.

The cosmic clues are evident when you pay attention to three things:

1. What you love,
2. What you're good at,
3. What you know is right for you. And when I say know, I mean that deep, cosmic, rock-solid *knowing* in your heart and soul that what you're doing, thinking or feeling is in alignment with the song in you.

The cosmic clues are often accompanied by what I call the cosmic goosebumps— when the hairs on your back or your arms raise up in acknowledgement that you are in the presence of something that resonates deeply with the song in you.

Now, I was lucky. I got the cosmic goosebumps when I was just a little sprout. They popped up every time I sang, danced, or otherwise hammed it up in front of one or more people—which, I'm told, I did continuously and without hesitation.

According to my earliest teachers, I had rhythm, and I danced with abandon. I loved music class at my bi-lingual kindergarten in Paris, France, where my dad, a diplomat in the US Foreign Service, was stationed. I learned to keep time, whacking little sticks or ringing little bells to images of musical beats on a large hanging banner. It was from that musically fertile environment that my aforementioned very first public performance—singing "She'll be Coming 'Round the Mountain" with my costumed classmates on a real stage—was spawned.

When I wasn't dancing or singing in school or at home, I was ordering my older brother, George, around (he nabbed cookies for me from the verbo-ten cookie jar) and pouting a great deal (signs of a truly great diva nature).

George even dubbed me "Triangle Mouth" for the way my lips pursed when I pouted. As I got older, my mother took to calling me "Tallulah," after Tallulah Bankhead, the great, dramatic —and extremely controversial—actress. This was perhaps because I was developing my propensity for exhibiting great swaths of divergent emotions—fantastic bouts of joy along with equally consuming tirades of wrath. I was a whirling dervish of emotions (and, I admit, I still am—just ask Jim, my hubby).

When I was six or seven, and living in Rome, Italy, I fell in love with an Italian singer named Rita Pavone. I watched her show on TV every week, waiting on pins and needles for her red-headed, false-eyelashed, mini-skirted, freckle-faced self to take the stage with her go-go booted backup dancers, and sing pop songs in Italian and adorably accented English. I absolutely wanted to be Rita Pavone; and so I hounded my parents into buying me two of her LPs, which I spun endlessly on my little red plastic record player. I sang and danced along with Rita for hours, much to my family's chagrin, embedding the songs in my soul to such a degree that more than forty years later, I can still recall them, word for word. Rita taught me to sing blues-based rock and roll, embrace being goofy, and turn slow ballads into heart-grabbing showstoppers.

Running a close second to my obsession with Rita Pavone was a television show curiously called *Il Zecchino D'Oro*, (The Golden Toothpick), a kind of pre-*American Idol* for children in which talented little kids from all over Italy sang original songs while looking cute, hoping to be crowned the winner. The *Zecchino D'Oro* songbook sold in the local magazine kiosk in advance of the show. Of course, I got one. I sang along with the kids, wishing in my little diva heart of hearts that it was me up there on that fuzzy black and white TV screen, singing to the masses. I remember those songs, too, and still have my *Zecchino D'Oro* songbook, messily marked up with colored pencils.

Adding to my musical education, my father, a colonel in the army in the Second World War, taught me army songs, which we would sing together in the car. Daddy, who had a lovely, deep baritone voice, tapped his wedding ring on the steering wheel, keeping time as we sang. He also substituted the words "ding de ding" for any unsavory words (of which there were many), as in:

"Put on that old blue ointment for the ding dings disappointment, keep it on for a week and a day... holy smokes how it itches, but it kills the ding de ding dings in the good old fashioned way...!"[2]

Further adding to my musical upbringing (not to mention my education in the ways of the world), was my beloved live-in au pair, Paola, an earthy, dark-eyed, twenty-year-old beauty from the Island of Sardinia, who lived with us. Paola insisted on teaching me Italian folk songs about cricket funerals and wildflowers, which we sang loudly together as we walked to the park every afternoon. Once there, she joined her buck-toothed and perpetually unemployed boyfriend, Luciano, at a prescribed park bench, where they immediately sat and enthusiastically made out. While they kissed, I hovered nearby, singing to myself as I swept the dirt floors of imaginary homes with tree branches.

I still have the words to the song about the cricket funerals, in Paola's hand-writing, in a diary from 1966. I took that diary, my precious records, my record player, and my Zecchino D'Oro songbook with me when my family was trans-ferred to Israel the summer of 1967, right before the Six Day War. It was in Israel that I fell over the edge into true diva-dom, declaring myself a budding thespian with a passion for the stage. It started rather innocuously, at Camp Haddassim, where I was sent for three interminable weeks during the summer of 1969.

OVER THE EDGE I GO
I am eleven years old.

Stuck in a bunk with three mean, spoiled little girls from New Jersey there to experience the wonders of the Holy Land and get out of their parents hair for the summer, I have never been so miserable. I long for my parents, my dog, Nino, and my troll doll, in that order. Tall and gangly, the round cheeks of my rear end poking out of my always-too-short one-piece bathing suits, wearing braces, pigtails, and handmade clothes, I do not blend well with the kids I am forced to bunk with. Tan and wiry, wearing the little, domed cotton sun hat typical of an Israeli, I look like a Sabra—a born and bred Israeli. The girls tease me mercilessly—for my homespun clothes, my seriousness, my lack of knowledge of American TV shows and, in particular, the fact that I still wear an undershirt instead of a training bra. As a result, I spend my camp days trying to phone my parents, avoiding my bunk mates, and flinging myself into every distraction I can possibly find, including basket weaving, glass blowing, and swimming (where my two, too-short bathing suits pale by comparison to my roommate, Sharon Sheinbaum's, endless parade of one and two-piece confections, each matching a different pair of Keds sneakers).

One afternoon, I get wind that there is going to be a Friday night talent show on the camp's big outdoor stage. Without any hesitation, I sign up to sing a song, despite the fact that I will be singing solo—and without musical accompaniment—in front of a big audience for first time in my life.

I spend the rest of the week trying to come up with the ideal song. Having accumulated a tiny collection of records in English by American musical artists, thanks to the record bin at the Post Exchange at the American Embassy, I have a bit of a repertoire from which to choose. I seriously consider two rather dramatic, bloodthirsty, weapon-ridden songs by cowboy singer Frankie Laine: "Wanted Man" and "Bowie Knife." But I finally settle on a less gory traditional folk song called "Froggy Went a Courtin."

I fling myself into preparing for my performance, painstakingly writing out the song lyrics in the pages of my camp diary and slipping away to rehearse behind trees and empty bunkhouses at every opportunity.

On the night of my performance, I carefully choose my costume—my best plaid dress, ordered from the Sears catalogue. Then I do something unprecedented: I let down my ubiquitous pigtails. My hair flows down my back. I feel glamorous, grown up, and positively diva-esque.
I walk to the wings of the camp's outdoor stage.

My heart is pounding in my chest.
BAM! BAM! BAM!
All of a sudden, Mr. Frankl, the camp leader, a native of Germany, speaks into
a scratchy microphone:

"Ladies und Gentlemen! From Bunk Eight, Eleni Kelakos vill now sing 'Frog
Vent a Courtin'! Let us give her a big hand!"

The sound of applause fills the air.

I step into a pool of light in the center of the stage.

I hear people breathing in the darkness, beyond the light. But I can't see them.

A fat, silver microphone perched on a rickety stand catches my attention. I step
to face it, drawn like metal to a magnet.

Taking a breath, I square my shoulders, and begin to sing. My voice rings out,
surprisingly loud: "Frog went a courtin' and he did go, uh huh."

And the audience replies, "Uh huh!"

What? Audience participation? Who knew?

I try another line: "Frog went a courtin' and he did go, uh huh."
The audience sings again, "Uh huh!" Their response is even louder than before,
a tidal wave of warmth that lifts me high.

Grinning like crazy, I finish out the verse: "Frog went a courtin' and he did go to
the Coconut Grove for the midnight show, uh huh, uh huh, uh huh!"
Now the audience is clapping along to the rhythm of the music.
Goosebumps on my naked arms!

My eyes have adjusted to the bright stage lights, and I can now make out some of
the faces beaming up at me. There's my nice counselor, Devorah, bopping and

bouncing along to my singing. There's my usually mean and snotty roommate, Sharon, looking at me like I used to look at Rita Pavone singing on TV, with a mixture of envy and admiration. And there, sitting like a queen, on a lawn chair in the very center of the audience, is Ma. Her proud smile feels like a big kiss. Could this moment be any sweeter? I don't think so.

I sing four more verses in a haze of glory.
When I'm done, the audience screams and applauds.

I blow a kiss, take my best diva bow: "Thank you, darlings!"

I step off the stage and into the audience. Hands reach up, pat my shoulder. Kids I barely know say "Nice job! Great voice!"

A really cute boy asks me to sit next to him on the grass!

Applause AND cute boys? Now that's a heady combo!
And that's when it happens: The performing bug zeroes in on my heart and chomps down, hard. I am hooked for life to the world of the stage.

I have found my path.

....

POINTS TO PONDER

Eleni finds her path, her passion and purpose, and lives happily ever after, yes?

Well, let's not get ahead of ourselves.

What I really want to point out here is that by naturally and intuitively following the cosmic clues, by paying attention to what I *love*, what I'm *good* at, and what I *know* is right for me, I ran smack dab into my unique passion and purpose (or soul role, as I like to call it). I say unique, because I believe there are as many passions and purposes as there are people. You're utterly unique, are you not? There's not another person on earth exactly the same as you. And so it stands to reason that your passion and purpose are tailor-made for you. It's just a matter of being conscious enough of the cosmic clues to recognize them.

Sometimes the cosmic clues are all around you, but you're not ready to notice them. For example, there's a young man I know. He sings and sings and sings. He sings when he's happy, when he's sad, when he's taking out the garbage. For all I know, he was singing in his mother's womb. He's like a walking, talking ipod. He knows the melody and lyrics to practically every song on the radio—rap, classic rock, easy listening, you name it. He has fantastic pitch and a beautiful, melodious voice. When he's not singing to himself, he's listening to music, downloading song after song.

Yet this young man—a twenty-three-year-old college senior—scratches his head a lot, wondering what the heck he's here to do in this lifetime. Should he be a sociology major or a broadcasting major? A psychology major or an English major? So far, he has yet to put two and two together and think, *Hey! Maybe I should explore a career that has something to do with music! I love music!*

Interestingly enough, he's never (as of this writing) been in a choir, a band, or a play. He's never even played an instrument, though he was given a guitar as a gift and the promise of a few lessons, which he's never pursued. He stays well away from the cosmic clues that are exploding all around him telling him, "Music! Music! Music!" He's just not ready to see them and, frankly, to follow where they may lead.

When you become conscious of the cosmic clues and start getting a sense of what you're here to do, there really is no going back.

PASSION VS. PURPOSE (2 OF THE 5 P'S)

Passion and purpose rule my life and my work, whether I'm standing on a speaking platform delivering a motivational presentation or working on a presentation with a coaching client. Passion and purpose are the first, foundational elements of what I call the Primary P's: Passion, Purpose, Preparation (getting and being ready), Planning (charting your course), and Persistence (taking consistent action that moves you forward in pursuing why you are here).

Loosely defined, passion is a strong and compelling feeling. If you look around, you'll notice just about everyone feels a passion for something, whether it be cooking, teaching high school, working with numbers, raising kids, or being creative. Paying attention to what you are passionate about—to what fires up your soul—leads you to your purpose.

PASSION

I happen to be an extremely passionate person, visibly passionate and enthusiastic about many things, not the least of which are music, acting, writing, personal growth (for myself or others), women's empowerment, speaking to or performing for groups, cooking and eating great food, and experiencing mind-blowing art. As I am constantly telling my coaching clients, passion is catching. When you're passionate, it stirs up passion in others, engaging their hearts and minds and catalyzing action.

Passion comes in all shapes, sizes, and forms. It can drive a vocation or an avocation. For example, I live in Ann Arbor, Michigan, where many people are passionate about the University of Michigan football team, the Wolverines. My neighbor has such a passion, in a big, big way. His passion drove him to buy the condo next door to me, even though he and his wife actually live four states away for most of the year. He did this just so he would have somewhere to stay within ten minutes drive of the UM stadium during football season. His car has license plates honoring his beloved team. The pots holding the plants in his front yard sport a telltale blue M for Michigan. He (and his very understanding family) gets up at the crack of dawn on football Saturdays so they can host fabulous tailgate parties and enjoy every morsel of a day defined by pigskin and massive, grunting guys in shoulder pads. There is no question in my mind that my neighbor is blessed with a deep, deep passion—one that moves me—a non-football fan—to actually give a hoot about the University of Michigan team, whenever I chance to speak with him about his passion. As I said, passion is catching.

PURPOSE (A.K.A. YOUR SOUL ROLE)

Purpose, on the other hand, is an aim or intention that guides your actions. It's *why* you do what you do. For example, I know that my purpose is to use the song in me to help other people stand out with confidence, clarity, and authenticity in their lives, their work, and their presentations. I use my personal passions, talents, and abilities—singing; writing songs, poetry, and prose; empathizing with and motivating others; telling stories; and empowering women—to support my greater purpose.

When you're near or around your purpose, it feels good, like you've come home to some place familiar and right. When you're engaged in your purpose, time flows easily and joyfully (just as it does when you're engaged in your passion).

Your core purpose (or soul role, as I also like to call it) remains a consistent thread throughout your life. The type of delivery method you use to express your purpose can, however, change many times, just as your passions can change. The delivery method of my purpose, for example, has changed several times over the years. I've morphed from actress, to singer, to songwriter, to workshop leader, to coach, trainer, professional motivational speaker, and author. But no matter what delivery method I've chosen, my core purpose has remained the same: To elevate and empower others.

When we start to become conscious of the cosmic clues, and begin to let them lead us down our unique life paths, we often have an abundance of passion, coupled with an increasingly defined purpose. The other P's—Preparation Planning, and Persistence—generally come later.

Your passion and your purpose work together, like a well-oiled machine. Passion drives purpose. Purpose without passion is like an engine without fuel. Yet all the passion in the world won't get you anywhere—at least anywhere specific—if you don't have a clear and compelling purpose.

KNOW THYSELF

As I continuously remind my coaching clients, great actors, great presenters, great leaders and conscious, realized people follow the first commandment of great acting and presenting: Know thyself.

So, what about you? How well do you know yourself? What do you love? What are you good at? When it comes to the core aspects of your life, what do you *know* is right for you to feel, think or do? What's your passion? What's your purpose? What cosmic clues have led you to them, or do you think might be leading you to them? You are here for a purpose. What is that purpose? My hope is this book will either help you find it or reassure you that you already have. Either way, congratulations on moving forward in your life!

SAY "AAA" (ATTITUDE, ACTION, ACCOUNTABILITY)
On a separate piece of paper, answer the following questions and complete the suggested exercises:

ATTITUDE
• What do you think or believe about your unique passion and purpose? How are you willing to change any negative thoughts or beliefs that might be keeping you from realizing your passion or purpose?

• What affirmation can you create, repeat, and embrace to help you maintain a more positive attitude about your passion and purpose (e.g., "I accept and honor my unique purpose.")?

ACTION

1. *Define Your Passion:* What are your special talents and abilities? What do you love to do? What are you good at? What, when you're around it or doing it, do you know is right for you? What gives you the "cosmic goosebumps?"

2. Look back at your life and list the cosmic clues, the defining "ah hah!" moments that have shaped your path so far. How willing are you to pay attention to—and follow—your cosmic clues?

3. *Define Your Purpose:* What do you think you're ultimately and uniquely on this planet to do? Write it down where you can find it, read it and remember it.

4. If you were to create a brief slogan that described the essence of your purpose (e.g., 'Helping Others Heal" or "Catalyst in Chief") what would it be?

5. What *one* action step will you take this week to honor your passion and your purpose?

ACCOUNTABILITY

What will you do/what system of accountability will you put into place to help yourself complete this week's action step?

CHAPTER TWO

The Lure of the Basement, the Call of the Stage: From Caterpillar to Butterfly

Ask the butterfly, as he flutters by, as he dances in the Spring
How he learned to float, like a crystal boat, on his richly jeweled wings,
and he'll say:
"Once I crawled on bended knees, clinging hard to trembling leaves,
Then I spun a cloak of dreams, now look at me: I can touch the sky..."
—ELENI KELAKOS, "TOUCH THE SKY" FROM *TOUCH THE SKY*

At the age of sixteen I got my first guitar. I'd been playing my brother George's prized Flamenco guitar, obsessively, for months, and he'd grown weary of hounding me to give it back. And so he convinced my parents to buy me my own. Early Christmas morning, when my pajama-clad brother marched into the living room strumming a tune on a classical guitar I'd never seen before, I was momentarily baffled: *Did George get another guitar?* Then George grinned and held the guitar out to me "Yours," he said, "Merry Christmas." I screamed for joy and leaped to my feet. Holding out my arms, I welcomed

my guitar with the eagerness and awe of a new mother greeting her baby
for the very first time. Ooh-ing and ah-ing, I noted the instrument's elegant
mother-of-pearl inlays, the lacquered smoothness of its wood, and the whimsical ring of rosewood butterflies fluttering around its soundhole. When I ran
my fingernails across its nylon strings, the guitar's reverberant, rich sound
kicked loose something deep within me. I fell in love at first strum.

I happily retreated with my guitar to the basement of our home in Canton,
Massachusetts, sitting on the steps, where the acoustics were particularly
good. My brother, an excellent guitarist, had taught me a few basic chords.
I put them together, figuring out how to play the traditional folk songs of The
Brothers Four or Burl Ives I'd learned in my early childhood as well as the songs
of pop artists like James Taylor and Janis Ian that were blasting on AM radio.

Singing along to my own guitar was much different than singing along to someone else's piano accompaniment, which I'd been doing in school musicals
and choirs since my summer camp talent show epiphany. I loved the challenge
of interpreting and expressing someone else's music and lyrics through the
vessel that was me. But the experience of strumming the strings of a resonant
box, and joining the sounds it made with my voice, moved me in a different
way. When I held and played my guitar, it felt as if music poured directly from
my soul.

One day, while I was noodling around on my guitar, safely ensconced in my
basement hideaway, I began to absentmindedly hum a melody along with a
simple series of chords. The hummed melody gave way to words: "Life is so
lovely when you're in love." Those eight words intuitively felt like the final,
anchoring lyrics of a musical chorus. I quickly captured those lyrics on a scrap
of paper. And when I did, it was as if I'd flung open the door to the Land of
Creation: A torrent of words and melodies came tumbling out, clamoring
to be claimed and noted. For half an hour, I scribbled and sang, scribbled
and sang. Before I knew it, I'd completed a chorus and three verses. When I
stitched together the verses and the chorus, and sang them out loud to the
basement walls, there was no mistaking what the echo of my voice revealed:
I had written a song.

I sang my new song over and over again, marveling how the melody and lyrics fit so neatly together. I'd never written lyrics before, though I'd tried my hand at poetry with some success. And I'd always easily expressed myself through the written word, as evidenced by the cosmic goosebumps that popped up when I wrote essays and short stories for school. English classes had always been a joy for me, no effort at all, an easy A; and my ninth grade English teacher, Mr. Bloom, had told me in no uncertain terms that I had the kind of verbal and writing skills that could eventually earn me a living. So I wasn't particularly surprised at my aptitude for writing lyrics. But I was surprised at the delicious feeling of power and ownership I felt marrying my singing voice with words and melody that sprung from my very soul. Experiencing the act felt sacred, precious, and deeply personal.

Out of respect for this feeling, I kept my song to myself, singing it in the basement, day after day, at the top of my lungs, to an audience of cobwebs and dust bunnies. I felt absolutely no desire to share it. I preferred cocooning in the basement like a caterpillar, hiding and protecting my budding talents— the song in me, literally and figuratively—in the safety and the privacy of the basement.

But then, all of a sudden, one spring afternoon, as I crooned away on the basement stairs, I heard it: I heard the song of my soul, whispering, insistent. A tiny voice, but strong and clear, coming from somewhere inside of me—my head, my heart, I couldn't tell: "Could be more," it said. "You could sing for the world."

I could sing for the world? Cool!

And then it hit me: If I wanted to sing for the world, I'd have to get out of the basement.

I had a choice: I could choose to hide in the basement, and keep my song all to myself, or I could choose to share it with others. Put another way: I could choose to make myself—and the song in me—smaller, or, to use an expression I use with my clients and audiences, I could choose to touch the sky.

DON'T TOOT YOUR OWN HORN

Stay in the basement? Or leave the basement?

This was an interesting dilemma for a girl raised by a strict, Greek-American dad with an unspoken girls handbook that contained the following set of rules:

1. Shut Up
2. Don't Talk Back
3. Don't Rock the Boat
4. Don't Toot Your Own Horn
5. And for Heaven's Sake, Be a Nice Girl!

Little did I know that most of these rules were reality for many girls of my generation (and the generations that preceded us).

What I did know was that it was not particularly seemly for me to speak up on behalf of my own abilities or accomplishments. I certainly did not race up the basement stairs, explode into the living room brandishing my guitar, and insist that my parents listen to my new song. Oh, no, no, no. Too risky— too much tooting of my own horn.

Instead, I took tiny tentative steps up the stairs and into the world beyond the basement, beginning with taking my guitar to play rehearsal at school, and singing my song for my trusted friend, Paul Ciccotelli. Paul whooped and hollered over the song, and, baby impresario that he was, actually asked to be my manager. His reaction tickled me to death, prompting me to run right back into the basement, where I wrote a whole passel of new songs. I shared those songs with Paul, several other buddies from the theatre club, and Mr. Lavache, the head of the music department, all of whom were very encouraging.

Slowly, leg by leg, I pulled myself out of my cocoon and risked showing the world beyond the basement my new, wet wings. It was both scary and exhilarating.

I unfurled my wings with abandon second semester, junior year, when, instead of submitting a series of original poems for a project in English class, I opted to hand in a series of original songs. As I earnestly explained to my teacher, Mr. Rich, my songs were poems set to music. I also requested permission to sing them to the class. Looking back at this, I see just how gutsy a move this was, flouting every rule in the girls handbook, by which I'd been raised.

Thankfully, Mr. Rich welcomed my hand-illustrated booklet of songs. And he gave me the green light for a classroom performance. And so I sang my now expanded canon of thirteen songs to my fellow classmates over the course of two class meetings. The kids were amazingly respectful and silent as I sang, and I was amazingly unafraid, my diva-ness prevailing. When I was through, and my classmates broke into spirited applause, I was awash and a-tingle with cosmic goosebumps.

Along with the "A" Mr. Rich gave me for the assignment, he included the following note:

"I have taught for the past nine years, and I have never enjoyed a class as much as the two classes in which you sang your songs to us. You have a rare talent, which I hope you continue to pursue. I hope that you have learned something about poetry and writing this year. I know that I have learned a good deal from you."

Reading Mr. Rich's comments, and recalling the enthusiasm with which my classmates had received my songs, I wondered: *Maybe the little voice in me was right. Maybe—just maybe—I really could sing for the world.*

THE LURE OF THE STAGE

My love affair with my guitar and my newly acquired passion for songwriting (all cosmic clues) neatly dovetailed with my passion for acting and performing. I'd already spent some of the happiest hours of my life playing leading roles in half a dozen school musicals and plays, sung challenging solos in school and community choirs, and had once even scored a part in a children's educational series on Israeli TV. I lived for the moments I performed for the public, loving everything from the rehearsals to the process of striking or tearing down a set. All the cosmic clues pointed unmistakably to a life on the stage.

Mr. Byk, an off-Broadway actor and my ninth grade drama director at the American International School in Israel, had once told me "You could be a professional actress—now put that in your back pocket and sit on it for a while." I had sat on his comment, for three whole years. But now high school graduation loomed and plans needed to be made. So I pulled Mr. Byk's long ago directive out of my pocket, ready to act on it.

I conferred with my current high school theatre director, Dick Rousseau, who was as passionate a theatre hound as I, and also with Mr. Ringuette, my guidance counselor. "Where should I go to college," I wondered, "if I wanted to study theatre?"

As a bright, perfectionistic, grade-grubbing student, who felt it was her duty to bring home straight A's on her report card, I had an excellent grade point average and SAT scores. This led Mr. Ringuette to suggest I try for the Ivy Leagues, specifically Dartmouth, Yale, and Brown (which was newly accepting women, and only a forty-five minute drive away). Mr. Rousseau, on the other hand, suggested Boston University, which, at the time, had a world-class theatre program.

I dutifully applied to all of them, mailing the envelopes off with crossed fingers and a prayer.

I had secret, special prayers for my application to Boston University, which was a real theatre school, not a liberal arts college like the others. B.U. required a challenging, day-long audition, which included preparing and presenting two contrasting monologues and a song, as well as participation in a dance class. I worked on my monologues all by myself, in the basement (of course). I had absolutely no idea whether I was performing them with any skill. But I was thrilled beyond belief at the chance to audition for people who could help me refine my abilities and point me down a professional path.

The day of the audition was a joyous blur. I remember looking and feeling like an elongated grape in my purple Danskin tights and leotard, as I leaped and flexed in a group dance class. I recall meeting a shimmering and exotic actress named Clarissa Bullitt, who sported a small, tinkling bell on a long silver chain and gave a heartbreaking rendition of Ophelia's dying monologue from Shakespeare's *Othello*. I remember the head of the school telling us that only sixty people out of several hundred applicants would be admitted to the program, and that of those sixty, only a handful would survive the full four years. And finally, I remember my audition, and the kind words uttered by one member of the panel of judges: "You're like a diamond in the rough. You need a lot of work, but there sure is a lot to work with."

After my audition at B.U., there was nothing more to do but wait and wonder which of the schools I'd applied to would welcome me. Every day, I scurried to the mailbox looking for fat letters of acceptance or thin letters of rejection from the five colleges in whose hands my future rested. I was ready to burst from the basement, and leap out into the greater world. But was the world ready for me?

....

POINTS TO PONDER

The Value of Cocooning: A Time to Sow, a Time to Reap

The song in you (your unique passion and purpose), is a sacred and vulnerable thing. It needs time, patience and tender loving care to develop from crawling caterpillar to winged butterfly. It relies on you to protect and nurture it, particularly during the early phases of determining its parameters.

Which is why, as you begin to put your arms around your unique passion and purpose, you must take care: Be wary of opening yourself up to potentially damaging judgment from others that you might not yet be strong enough to handle. Cocooning, whether literally in the basement, as I did, or tucked into a safe corner of your home or office where there are no harsh judging eyes and ears, is part of the process of developing and ultimately trusting your own voice.

Shifting back and forth from the basement to the world beyond it is a natural part of the creative process and of the flow of life. I always retreat to "the basement" every time I embark upon a new project. I think of it as planting— or sowing—seeds, and then giving those seeds the time and the nurturing they need to grow deep roots and gather strength and energy—strength and energy they'll need to break through the earth's crust and touch the sky.

That's why I don't share a new song, a new presentation, or a new business idea with anybody until I've worked it through to my own satisfaction. This book, for example, didn't grace anybody's eyes but mine during its initial stages, except select members of my hand-picked backup choir (more about the value of selecting a great choir in chapter seven), such as my personal coach, Mark Le Blanc, and my husband, Jim. At the writing stage, my goal was to tap into and follow the cosmic clues and the little voice inside me, letting them nudge my written words into existence. I took my manuscript out of the basement eventually, opening it up to the judgment of others (like a professional editor), but only after I allowed its authentic core to form itself on my computer screen in the safety and privacy of my office.

When it comes to the song in you, your own particular passion, purpose, talents, dreams, and desires, you are the best judge of when to quietly nurture and strengthen it, and when to begin to move up the basement stairs and out the door into the world. Like a butterfly, you'll have been growing and developing within your cocoon. The cocoon will start to feel confining, and you'll strain against it, wanting to move beyond its limits. The little voice in you will grow louder and louder, urging you to trust that you're ready to reap what you've sown, ready to share what you have been developing so you can find the people who are looking for just what you have to offer. Some of us are born ready. Some of us need a little more time to get ready. And that's ok.

What is important is that you take the time you need to take to develop the song in you in the safety and security of the basement, and that, when you heed the call to move beyond it, you are willing to take that first step up and out—even if you're scared beyond measure.

SAY "AAA"

On a piece of paper, write your responses to the following questions, and complete the exercises:

ATTITUDE

• What were the unspoken messages you received in your upbringing about standing out, speaking out, or achieving? How do they affect your attitude today?

• What affirmation can you create, repeat, and embrace to help you maintain a more positive attitude (e.g., "I am willing to stand out in all my fabulousness!" or "I have a lot to say and the courage to say it!")?

ACTION

1. What stage of development of your voice are you in? Are you cocooning and keeping your unique talents or gifts all to yourself while you develop, nurture, and define them? Or are you ready to exit the basement, unfurl your wings, and share the song in you with the world?

2. What do you need to do to feel ready to exit the basement and share the song in you with others?

3. Create a set of new rules for yourself that reflect your unique philosophy, an expanded, hopeful outlook, and room for the song in you to blossom. Post your new rules somewhere you can read them daily.

4. Write down *one* action step you will take this week to move up and out of the basement so you can share the song in you with others.

ACCOUNTABILITY
What will you do/what system of accountability will you put into place to help yourself complete this week's action step?

CHAPTER THREE

Shrinking to Fit

"Rules and Regulations in the Poppy Land
Made it clear to Petal that growing tall was bad.
Don't grow past your neighbors
Was the Final Word…"
—ELENI KELAKOS, "THE TALLEST POPPY," FROM *TO THE BONE*

One by one, college acceptances and rejections began to roll in. Yale didn't want me. Dartmouth College wait-listed me. Brandeis University wanted me and threw in some money to prove it. Brown University absolutely wanted me. But, most importantly, at least for me, Boston University wanted me. Oh rapture, oh joy! I still have the letter of acceptance, and it still thrills me when I read it.

My parents were ecstatic, particularly about my acceptance to Brown University. As far as my dad was concerned, this was a dream come true: His daughter, an Ivy League student! As a pragmatic scientist, an M.I.T. graduate, with a not-so-far-in-the-past blue-collar childhood in hardscrabble Lowell, Massachusetts, there was no question in Dad's mind what school I should attend.

As far as I was concerned, however, what really mattered was that Boston University had accepted me into their theater program. This affirmed my belief that I was meant to have a professional career as an actress and that I really was a diamond in the rough worthy of polishing, as the folks on the audition panel had implied. I wanted to go to B.U. with all my heart and soul.

My father, who was paying the bills, kept nudging me firmly towards Brown. "You're a good student," he said. "Study more than just theatre. Stretch your brain. You can always do theatre on the side at Brown." I understood the logic behind Daddy's reasoning. And I appreciated his faith in my intellect, as well as his desire to provide me with an excellent, well-rounded education. Still, B.U. pulled at my heart.

One night, in the throes of deciding between Brown and B.U., I happened to overhear my parents talking in the living room.

"That girl has stars in her eyes," my father was saying. "Doesn't she know that other people are better than she is?"

I went to bed and cried myself to sleep. At breakfast, I announced I would go to Brown, period.

And just like that, I kicked the song in me back down into the basement and slammed the door so hard the house rattled. Wham!

Without so much as a whimper or a heated word on behalf of the song in me, I yielded in the face of an obstacle. I let somebody else's voice become more important than my own. I gave in to my tendency to shrink to fit—a tendency that had been seeded and nurtured in my home and, perhaps most earnestly, in the wild and wooly hallways of junior high school.

THE TALLEST POPPY

Junior high.

Just writing those words makes me want to call my therapist.
But there really is no way for me to write adequately about shrinking to fit without a side trip back to the seventh grade

I entered junior high school flying my freak flag with great and oblivious abandon. I was a nice, grade-grubbing, teacher-loving, rule-following theatre geek. And if that wasn't bad enough, I was also tall. I mean, really tall. Taller than the boys. The evidence is scattered throughout my dusty photo albums. In photo after photo, I loom above my friends like a lanky baby giraffe. After too many years of being yanked out of the front row by my teachers so I wouldn't block anybody from the camera's view, I got really good at knowing where to stand when the shutter snapped during the class photo: Off to the side, like a bookend. Or in the middle of the back row, head and shoulders poking out of the lineup, no matter how hard I tried to fit in.

But it wasn't until I went to my first junior high school dance that I realized my height could be a real obstacle—particularly when it came to attracting boys.

Dance with Me, Pleeeeeeeeeeeeeeeeeeeeeeease!

I'm wearing my best, skin-tight, Landlubber, hip-hugger jeans, that have been lengthened on the bottom with a strip of red, white, and blue denim. It is, after all, 1970, and I'm a little hippie girl. My hair is long and parted down the middle like every other girl in the seventh grade, and I'm wearing my brother's groovy gold peace sign pendant around my neck.

I'm dying to go to this dance, because, hey! I can dance! My friend Michelle's older sister Nancy has been showing me how. I've been practicing in front of my mirror every night, shaking my bony hips and wriggling my skinny arms like snakes. Oh yeah! Oh yeah! Oh yeah! I'm hot! I'm hot!

My mom drops me off at the dance. I walk into the packed gymnasium, bell-bottoms swishing. The lights are low. Sixties rock and roll blaring from the AV system: "In-A-Gadda-Da-Vida, baby...!"

I lean casually against the black-light posters taped to the walls, put a hand on my hip, throw my long hair back suggestively, and I wait. I wait. I wait.

For something to happen.

For someone to ask me to dance. Anyone.

Oh! Look! Across the dance floor! There's my friend Joni! She's dancing! Jeez, look at her go! Joni is blond. Blue-eyed. Cute.

And short.

Hey! There's my friend Ashley! Man, can she dance!

Ashley's been dancing all night, with boy, after boy, after boy.

Ashley is blond. Green-eyed. Cute.

And... well... short.

And now, the seconds, the minutes, the hours are just whizzing by, and nobody has asked me to dance. Nobody! Not one boy! Hot little tears gather behind my eyelids, my lower lip begins to quiver...

But wait! Striding confidently towards me, with a little glint in his eye, is Steven Whittington... Little Steven Whittington, no bigger than a minute... And he asks me to dance.

Now Steven is not exactly my ideal dance partner. But hey! He asked! He has cajones! And so I shrug, toss my hair back, first with one hand, and then the other, and I say, "Yeah."

And then he pulls me out to the dance floor, and he takes his chubby little hands and he presses them, hard, against my hair, so my head snaps back and my chest— such as it is—thrusts out in all its pubescent magnificence. And then he takes his happy, sweaty little face and he places it right there, smack dab in the middle of the two little humps formed by my Playtex junior miss double A brassiere.

And then we dance. To the longest slow song known to man, "Hey Jude," by the Beatles.

"Na na na na na, na na na nah....!"

And as I look down at the part on little Steven Whittington's head, I think, "Oh, please God, let it get better than this."

In that moment, I felt like the tallest poppy in the poppy field.

Which, if you know anything at all about the Tall Poppy Syndrome, is not a good thing. The Tall Poppy Syndrome, in case you're wondering, is a philosophy prevalent in Australia and New Zealand that goes something like this: If you're a poppy in a poppy field, you're not supposed to grow any taller than any of the other poppies. Metaphorically speaking, you're supposed to grow neck and neck, stem to stem, pistil to pistil, petal to petal, as tall—and no taller—than all the poppies in the field. In other words, *don't stand out.*

And if you *do* stand out, woe betides you because, as Steve Carrell's character, Barry, said in the movie *Dinner for Schmucks*, "The tallest people get chopped down first."[3]

Don't stand out. Easier said than done when you're an extremely tall, extraverted, theatre geek diva with a tendency to be just a wee bit melodramatic. I stood out just by standing up.

Still, I tried. I did my best to shrink to fit.

I wore flats. And I learned to schlump. I became, in fact, the queen of schlumping. My technique was simple: Thrust out a hip; lose a couple of inches. It was uncomfortable as hell, and made me walk like a dork, but, hey, for a few painful moments I felt like I was breathing the same air as the rest of the gang. But then, off I'd go to the mall to buy a pair of jeans and dang! Reality slapped me hard in the face—ankle-waders, every time.

I got the message early: You're just too tall. Actually, it was more like I was just too, too—too smart, too nice, too hard-working, too dramatic, too emotional—too Eleni.

When I think back to those formative years from junior high through the twelfth grade, I realize what I *really* had too much of was a tendency to be too passive, pleasing, and perfect, at my own expense. But, of course, I didn't see it that way at the time. I was too busy with the impossible task of trying to be passive, pleasing, perfect, and, generally speaking, in control of every single blessed thing around me. This included trying in vain to rein in my growing, changing body, which was softening with the rounded curves of early womanhood.

Because my parents were caught up in the ever-increasing drama of my dad's retirement, coupled with his diagnosis of Parkinson's disease, they didn't really notice I was getting smaller and smaller. Not just physically, but energetically and psychologically as well. Because literally shrinking to fit— dieting enough to make me stop having menstrual periods for a whole year and shedding hair like an oak tree dropping leaves in the fall—was only one manifestation of my willingness to make myself small. I was, in truth, shockingly willing to tamp down my mighty emotions, pooh-pooh my sharp mind, downplay my overflowing enthusiasm, swallow my opinions, and sweep my needs and desires under the carpet.

And my burgeoning sensuality? I slapped that aside, thank you very much. Especially after the remark my dad made when I chortled, once, at a dirty joke on late-night television: "Honey," he said, shaking his head, "What happened to you? You used to be so sweet?" At the time I was, may I point out, a senior in high school.

I got the message. My job was to be passive, be perfect, and to please others, even at my expense. And to absolutely not rock the boat. So I didn't. At least not for a good, long time. I became the perfect parts car.

ON BEING A PARTS CAR

A parts car, literally speaking, is a car whose parts—a muffler, a right rear door—are used to help other cars work or look better.

People can be parts cars, too.

"Parts Car-itis"—otherwise known as "Doormat-itis"—is a condition common to people who are strongly compelled to put their needs dead last and give, give, give unto others until it hurts. As a parts car, you willingly sacrifice your physical and mental resources at the altar of someone else. Bit by bit, part by part, you give away the best parts of yourself—including the song in you—to help someone else function better, look better, feel better, or feel bigger. And then you wonder why your stripped down, sorry self is stuck and stalled on the side of the road, unable to move ahead.

Women have been both willing and unwilling parts cars probably since Neanderthal times. I can hear the typical cavewoman now:

"It's ok, dear. Go hunting for three months, and leave me alone with winter coming and our six kids and the gathering and the cooking and the cleaning of the cave and the sewing of the pelts, and the looking after your mother and your three menopausal aunts. I was going to sign up for a month-long basket weaving class over at the next cave, because I really do feel I have a knack for it, but that can wait. It's certainly not nearly as important as you going after that big old mastodon, my sweet and hairy angel."

I learned how to be a parts car from a master: My mother, Theresa. I learned so well that I'm still unlearning it.

Ma was a formidable force of nature, a visual artist who could take any sort of medium—oil paints, clay, cloth, thread, a pencil and paper—and create indelible works of art, often loaded with vibrant and whimsical color. She taught me to believe I could create anything I saw in my head, and so I did (and still do). Ma had a wild, creative, and impulsive nature that was present, in particular, when my father was not around or when she was immersed in creating her art. I had a glimpse of Ma's messy, bohemian side as a little girl, when she took me to her oil painting class in Rome. In that setting, I was, for once, not Ma's complete focus. I was left to wander and watch, as Ma, in a pink, paint-spattered smock, surrendered to the canvas in front of her, flushed, focused, exuberant. Her flamboyant teacher, Mr. Maione, stepped in, from time to time, to steer her paintbrush—his arm in an easy arc around her shoulders—and to whisper instructions in broken English. The air shimmered with sound, smells—the scritch-scratch of bristles on canvas, the warm scent of linseed oil. It was intimate, exuberant, and downright sensual. I loved it. I loved seeing Ma so fully present and so joyfully in command of her artistic expression.

But then the class ended, and all evidence of messy, bohemian Mom got packed away in her wooden paint box. Not a spot of paint on her skin or her clothing. Not an errant brush, used rag, or can of turpentine within view. Back at home, Ma once again became the perfectly attentive, groomed, and per-fumed diplomat's wife, hustling to change into a fresh dress before Daddy arrived for dinner.

At the dinner table, Ma served herself dead last and always took the least appealing pork chop or cut of meat. My father often led the conversation, and my mother never contradicted him, never argued, never talked back. If he criticized her ("No, Theresa, you're wrong! What you are saying is *not* accurate!"), she'd simply shut up, shut down, and rip her paper napkin into little pieces.

Ma never gave herself permission to let her passion and talent for art take precedence over her real duties—being the passive, pleasing, and perfect wife and mother, so typical of her generation.

How I wanted Ma to give the song in her some room to breathe and grow. I wanted her to have vacations, time off from caring for my increasingly sick dad, fun, friends, and fulfillment. But most of all, I wanted her to have a room of her own, a studio devoted to her art that she'd never have to pack away. After many years (and much therapy), I now understand that what I really wanted was for Ma to give herself permission to let her art—the song in her—lead out, so I could feel free to do the same.

As an eighteen-year-old living in my father's house, and as a dutiful parts car, like my mother, I had neither the voice nor the courage to speak up passionately on behalf of my artist's soul and claim my right to attend Boston University's theatre school.

And so, along with my other essentials—writing journal, guitar, faded jeans, and Olympia manual typewriter—I packed my tendency to shrink to fit into the powder blue luggage that accompanied me to Perkins Hall dormitory at Brown University in the fall of 1976.

POINTS TO PONDER

Are you a parts car? How much of the song in you—your dreams, your opinions, your desires, your abilities—have you been willing to give away? How willing are you to reclaim and re-connect who you really are so you can lead the life you deserve to live?

At an initial meeting, a potential client, the president of a public relations firm, looked up at me with tears in her eyes and said, "Help! I've lost myself!" I hear variations of this anguished statement time and time again with coaching clients as well as audience members. Whether they are talking about their lives, their work, or their presentations skills, the pain and the point is the same: These people—primarily women—are feeling lost, unmoored and adrift from the core elements of their authentic selves. They've gotten into the habit of being a parts car. They've given away their right to shine. And it's killing them. They're great at nurturing others, but lousy at taking care of themselves and honoring the song in them. They're uncomfortable around conflict, and so they shut up and shut down instead of voicing their opinion. They don't want to rock the boat, or risk not being liked, so they stay mute, mum, mild. Over time, the song in them gets so soft, so small, that they can barely hear it anymore.

Take a creative, capable woman I'll call Sandra, who runs the marketing department at a major corporation. On top of an already massive workload, she's also been quietly doing the job of one of her male colleagues because he is, apparently, incapable of doing it himself. In spite of the undercurrent of resentment she feels doing his work for him and watching him get the credit for it, she still gives her precious time and energy away to help him look good (and, as she explains, maintain the bottom line of her department) rather than let him falter and fail by his own hand. Sandra is often exhausted and overburdened by a life dictated by the constant ringing of not one but two cell phones; a life that spins out of control because she's still learning how to say no to others and yes to herself. Juggling work, travel, the crazy after-school schedules of two growing kids, and a marriage, Sandra has very little time for her own needs. One morning when she was getting her son ready for school, she reminded him to eat a good breakfast so he'd be fueled up for the day. "I will if you do," he said, knowing that his mom rarely, if ever, ate breakfast before launching out the door to start her marathon days. Ouch! Out of the mouths of babes...!

As Sandra is discovering in our work together, it takes clarity, courage, and will to maintain the boundaries necessary for your well-being. To protect the time and space you need to develop yourself and your work, you must learn to say yes to your needs and no to others'.

Women are, frankly, lousy at saying no. We capitulate quickly and easily in the face of opposition, not wanting to offend or to be disliked. As a result, all too often (and all too easily), we let ourselves—and the song in us—down, by allowing others (even well-meaning others) to trample all over the boundaries we've painstakingly erected.

WOULD YOU MIND...?

My friend Lorel, a fabric artist, began taking Wednesdays off from her day job so she could enjoy one full day devoted to her creative work. Initially, she was thrilled with the new arrangement and the creative freedom it gave her. Eventually, the decision became less rosy. One Wednesday morning, Lorel decided to look ahead towards dinner and prepare some spareribs for smoking—usually a simple job. But when she discovered she needed to clean the dirty smoker, what should have been a simple job turned into an ordeal that lasted three hours. Three whole hours stolen from the precious time she originally allotted towards making her art.

As Lorel later admitted, it's incredibly easy to get distracted (or distract herself) from what she needs to be doing. There's always something or someone that's going to brazenly step over the boundaries she's established and lure her away from what she's planned on doing. It often starts with her husband prefacing a sentence with, "Would you mind…?" As in, "Would you mind going to the dry cleaners on your way back from that client meeting?" or "Would you mind watering the plants when you get a minute?" If Lorel isn't vigilant, the precious hours she allocated for the care and development of her art get whittled down to nothing.

We need to learn from Lorel and be aware that people—even those who love us—will take advantage of us to the degree we let them. It is all too easy to give in to the tendency to care for others before caring for ourselves.

So, what about you?

How willing are you to speak your truth and express what you need? How far will you go to protect the song that is unique to you and lead the life you deserve to live?

It you have the tendency towards being a parts car, raise your right hand and repeat after me:

I solemnly swear
To honor myself
To honor the song in me
And not be a parts car!

There you go: You've now taken the Parts Car Oath. Honor it! Take owner-ship of who you are and what you're here to do. Step up to the plate and protect the boundaries you've established around what you love, what you're good at, and what you know is right for you. Protect those boundaries con-sciously and consistently, whether you're starting a new business, writing a book, or selling Silpada jewelry out of your spare bedroom. Remember, how you treat the song in you determines how others will treat it. So treat it with the respect that it—and you—deserves.

SAY "AAA"

On a piece of paper, write your responses to the following questions, and complete the exercises:

ATTITUDE

- Do you believe you have a right to shine? What is your general attitude about shrinking to fit so others can feel more comfortable around you?

- What affirmation can you create, repeat, and embrace to help you maintain a more positive attitude (e.g., "I joyously and willingly share my unique gifts with the world.")?

ACTION

1. Under what circumstance, or around what sort of person, do you tend to be a parts car? Conversely, when (in what situation, or around what sorts of people) are you most willing to shine?

2. Describe a situation in which you chose to play small. How did it make you feel?

3. What do you stand to gain by choosing not to play small?

4. How comfortable are you in the face of conflict? How willing are you to rock the boat in the name of your most compelling beliefs or the song in you?

5. Make a list of your unique and precious passions, talents, dreams, and desires. Circle the ones you are absolutely unwilling to give up, for any reason or for anybody. Are there any on your list you've already given away or abandoned? Any you need to reclaim or recover?

6. What *one* action step are you willing to take this week to encourage yourself to stop playing small?

ACCOUNTABILITY
What will you do/what system of accountability will you put into place to help yourself complete this week's action step?

CHAPTER FOUR

The Perils of Limbo

"When you keep one foot in the basement, and one foot out of the basement, you get absolutely nowhere."
—ELENI KELAKOS

I avoided the Brown University theatre department for the better part of a year—ironic for someone who'd been publicly dubbed "Canton's Gift to Broadway" by my high school principal when he handed me my diploma. Like a crack addict gone straight, I went cold turkey: No plays, no theatre classes, no auditions. Instead, I threw myself into exploring other disciplines—psychology, sociology, French.

I did let myself find a way to sing, however, because singing didn't officially qualify as acting, and, therefore, seemed safe. When I auditioned for the Brown University chorus, Bill Ermey, the exacting choral director, sounded out my voice on the piano and pronounced me good enough to sing in not one, but all three choirs. And so I sang challenging classical and contemporary pieces on small and large stages—including Alice Tully Hall at Lincoln Center in New York City—once even conducted by the great composer Aaron Copeland. I also sang a heady soprano solo in *Bruchner's Mass in G,* a scary but thrilling proposition.

I also joined a band called Windy Mountain, in which, coincidentally, a friend from Canton, Massachusetts, played electric guitar. I was hurrying to the college green, on my way to a student jam session, my guitar bouncing against my back, when he flagged me down, dragged me into a band rehearsal, and insisted I sing a song for his band mates. This impromptu audition immediately catalyzed two steady relationships: One with Dave, my first real boyfriend and the leader of the band, and the other with the band itself, singing lead vocals. The latter relationship gave me the chance to sing and play in lots of seedy bars under the most challenging of circumstances, teaching me crowd control techniques I still employ today.

I remember playing one club in particular, the HD (short for Harley Davidson) Pub, populated by big, hairy, scary looking, tattooed members of motorcycle gangs. They were huge fans of our music—country rock—and a surprisingly sweet and attentive audience. One of its toughest denizens, a bulky, weathered woman in her late forties, in leather from head to foot, swaggered up to me and stopped three inches from my face, breathing beer breath for what seemed an eternity. "I like your boots," she finally said, in a shockingly shy, little girl voice. We both looked down at my brand new pair of black leather boots and sighed with appreciation—fashion truly knows no boundaries. That same night, I remember going to the restroom and seeing "I love the chick singer" freshly scrawled on the dirty wall. Wow, cool! I was the "chick singer"! From the basement to the HD Pub! Now that was progress.

Being the chick singer in a band, singing in various choirs, juggling a heavy academic schedule, and having a serious boyfriend served as colossal distractions from the perpetual siren call of the theatre department, which I was resolved to avoid in honor of my father. I was still powerfully conflicted about what I loved doing (theatre and performing in general) and what I thought I should be doing (anything else).

I didn't take a class labeled TA (Theatre Arts) until the second semester, and then only because it seemed prim and benign, called, as it was, Voice and Diction. The class was taught by Professor Jim Barnhill, the head of the theatre department, who was anything but prim. His animated, bushy eyebrows, southern drawl, and great love of theatre made for a charming, compelling package. I loved working on and delivering the poems and mono-logues that comprised the meat of Jim's class, and I excelled, receiving the Mary Ellen Hicks award for elocution for my efforts.

Jim Barnhill recognized a diva when he saw one—even one who was trying to stay undercover. One spring day, he literally pulled me off the sidewalk and into his office. "You need to be in the theatre department!" he declared, slapping his desk, his eyebrows wriggling like fat centipedes. "You must take my studio acting class next semester!"

I agonized over whether to sign up for the class for several weeks. My internal voices sparred mightily. "No! Don't scratch that acting itch!" hissed one voice, sounding remarkably like my dad. Another, smaller, truer voice whispered, "Do it" (which was, coincidentally, Professor Barnhill's favorite expression). And so I finally did do it, signing up guiltily for what I knew was not just a class but a tacit understanding that I would be majoring in theatre arts.

ONE FOOT IN AND ONE FOOT OUT

If you are familiar with a song and dance called the Hokey Pokey, you will understand the dance I danced over my next three years at Brown: One foot in, and one foot out. Though, on paper, I initially declared myself a theatre major, I did it with a level of commitment that can only be described as lame. I just couldn't shake my dad's words ("That girl has stars in her eyes!") or the fact that my decision to go to Brown instead of Boston University had prompted both my brother and my best friend, Neil, to express their relief that I had apparently decided not to pursue acting as a profession. The unstated—and sometimes stated—opinion of close family members and friends was that dabbling in theatre was OK. Committing to a life on the stage was not. And even though I secretly believed the reverse—that committing to a life on the stage was exactly what a born diva like me should do—I still couldn't seem to muster up the courage to defy my family and stand by that belief.

And so I stayed stuck between what increasingly felt like two distinct sides: My father's, in which dabbling in theatre was preferred; and Professor Barnhill's, in which committing wholeheartedly to a life on the stage was a respectable choice worthy of my talents. The more I leaned towards my father's side, letting myself merely dabble in theatre arts, the more I longed for the deeper involvement in theatre represented by Jim Barnhill's side. The more I leaned towards Jim Barnhill's side, and outing myself as a bonafide actress, the more I felt I was risking my father's disappointment and disapproval. As a result, I lingered unhappily in a murky limbo that represented a third side—a side of mixed messages, in which my passion and abilities had merit, but only to a certain degree. I tried, in fact, to keep a lid on the exuberance or pride I felt when I received affirmation for my abilities as an actress and singer. When Jim Barnhill cast me in the lead role of the sultry scullery wench Aldonza in *Man of La Mancha*, for example, I let myself get excited for a few heady minutes. And then I wrenched the rug of happiness out from under my own feet by reminding myself that I was just lucky to have been cast. No matter that in order to attend callbacks I had to walk a mile through two feet of snow deposited by the famed Blizzard of '78, and still somehow sing and act my rear end off under enormous pressure. No matter that Professor Barnhill had believed in my abilities enough to choose me over a dozen qualified actresses. The night that *Man of La Mancha* opened, I remember waiting to go on, feeling that delicious mix of nerves and joyous anticipation, and then consciously squishing down those feelings of elation, telling myself that it was *only* a play. I wasn't going to let myself get swept up in the silly notion that theatre was my be-all and end-all. Because if I could convince myself that theatre wasn't important enough to pursue professionally, I might spare myself from being rejected not only by my father, but by the professional theatre community. After all, hadn't Daddy said, "Doesn't she understand that there are other people who are better than she is?" It never even dawned on me that it didn't matter how good I was compared to other actors. What really mattered was my willingness to be as good as I could be.

My parents came to see the show, which was both exciting and terrifying. I was, after all, playing a tempestuous whore: I wore a leather bustier that pushed my boobs up to my nose and got gang raped on stage by six bawdy muleteers who threw me over a trunk and smacked me with a bullwhip. Not exactly kid stuff. My father was, to put it delicately, aghast, though he did admit that I sang well. My mother gushed profusely over my performance, going so far as to kiss every single one of my cast mates in jubilation. Always a fan, she did love to see me on stage, particularly in musicals. Unfortunately, that's as far as her support went. As much as I would've liked for Ma to go head-to-head with my dad and publicly defend my desire to be an actress, it simply wasn't her place to do so. In keeping with her traditional upbring-ing, Ma genuinely believed that my father, as the man of the house, should have the final say on pretty much everything. Since I essentially followed my mother's lead, I figured if it wasn't Ma's place to contradict my father in support of my desires, it couldn't possibly be mine. It never dawned on me that I had the right to speak up for myself and fight my own battles.

I continued my maddening dance—one foot in the basement, one foot out. By the time I had to make a formal decision to declare my major (or concen-tration, as it's called at Brown), I had fretted myself into a corner. How could I be attending an Ivy League college and be a theatre major? That seemed, somehow, preposterous, especially with my father paying the bills. I so didn't want to disappoint Daddy. I finally settled the dilemma by declaring not one but two concentrations: One in theatre arts, the other in semiotics (don't ask, the semiotics professors didn't seem altogether sure of what it was all about either. But it did let me intern at a TV station and take advanced writing classes). Settling on two concentrations was another example of my inability to make a clear choice one way or the other, otherwise known as "neither-here-nor-there-itis."

Even though, on paper I was a theatre major, I pursued my theatre studies in a half-baked fashion, auditioning only when I felt I had a good shot at getting a part and not getting as utterly absorbed in the theatre department as many of my classmates—the so-called real actors, as I tended to think of them.

In spite of four semesters of actor training, countless hours of stage time, and several challenging singing and acting roles under my belt, I didn't consider myself a real actress. A real actress, I believed, would have launched herself into every audition and every play and every theatrically-oriented experience within her grasp (much as I had in junior high and high school). A real actress wouldn't run so hot and cold in acting class, doing top-of-the-line work one day (when I chose to be thoroughly focused and committed) and doing mediocre work the next (when I scrambled back to the basement again afraid of the consequences of committing too deeply). A real actress wouldn't be vacillating about whether or not to be an actress upon graduation, which was looming.

Jim Barnhill summed it all up nicely in the following written evaluation:

"Ms. Kelakos is a striking performer, and yet [she] seems unsure as to whether or not she should continue to pursue theatre as a career option."

No kidding.

Even after a triumphant experience playing the romantic lead in *Brigadoon* my senior year at Brown, I still didn't believe I had it in me to commit to being a professional actress. I had, in fact, no idea what the heck I was going to do when I graduated. Better put, I knew what I *wanted* to do; I just didn't feel I deserved to do it. In a meeting of senior theatre arts concentrators, when I was asked to reveal my plans for the future, I shrugged and flippantly said, "I don't know… maybe I'll go to L.A. and be the next Carol Burnett (my singing, acting, comedienne, sketch artist hero, at the time)." But even as I said it, I felt like a fraud.

To confuse the matter, I was excelling in (and truly enjoying) a journalism writing class taught by Debra Shore, the managing editor of the *Brown Alumni Monthly* magazine. Debra loved my writing and brought it to the attention of the editor-in-chief, who offered me a staff writing job upon graduation. I thanked him, told him I'd think about it, and left his office more confused than ever.

I did think about it and everything else related to what I might do in the big, bad world upon graduation. I thought and I thought and I thought. The more I thought, and the nearer I came to graduation, the more freaked out I became. I started literally having trouble getting out of bed in the morning. Frozen to the sheets, sweating, and bug-eyed, I was having what I now understand to be panic attacks. Somehow, I managed to get myself up and out to my classes and to my internship at PM Magazine at W|AR, Providence's primary television station. I told no one—absolutely no one, not my parents, not my teachers, not my family, not my friends, not my boyfriend—about the wretched mornings spent panicked and pinned under my bedclothes. It was my dirty little secret. I was, after all, supposed to be perfect.

Right around this time, Don Wilmeth, the new head of the theatre department, asked me to audition to be a part of the Brown University Summer Theatre's four-play season. The day of the auditions, I managed to talk myself into not going. After all, I reasoned, I wasn't a real actor, capable of handling four straight plays (non musicals). Besides, I was probably too tall (a point that Professor Barnhill had delicately broached as being a possible challenge in a professional acting world dominated by short men), and therefore not easily cast, especially in four, disparate plays. And so, I stayed, metaphorically, in the basement feeling sorry for myself.

This, by the way, is, I'm embarrassed to say, pretty much how I handled that lovely job offer from the editor-in-chief of the *Brown Alumni Monthly*: I just never gave him a final reply. And he never followed up with me wondering why I'd dropped off the face of the planet.

Don Wilmeth, on the other hand, would not let the matter rest, God love him. After the auditions, at which I'd simply not shown up, he sought me out, shook his finger in my face, and told me to never, ever again sabotage myself by deciding in advance how someone might or might not cast me. "I'm casting you anyway," he said, as he walked away, "even though you didn't audition." I was floored, not to mention humbled and grateful. I surprised myself—and without a doubt, my parents—by taking the job.

I was about to take one foot out of the basement.

TWO FEET IN

When I look at photos of me brandishing my diploma at graduation from Brown University in the spring of 1980, I look positively giddy. Not a trace of the anguish I'd been experiencing over the previous few months shows in my beaming face.

I was embarking on what would turn out to be one of the happiest summers of my life: A summer spent rolling around in one play after the next, in the company of a group of people I absolutely adored, all of us intent on making great art to the best of our ability.

Every day I woke up to my new life as a salaried actor, working with a smile and a happy heart. I spent my time learning what felt like an endless stream of lines, rehearsing one show by day and performing another at night. After the show, I hung out with the cast at various bars and taverns, drinking pitchers of beer, laughing, and discussing art, philosophy, life. It was grand. I couldn't believe I was being paid to have such a good time.

One of my all-time greatest, fondest memories of that summer still makes my heart sing:

It's a late summer morning, and I've been released from rehearsal for a lunch break. But I'm not interested in the sandwich I made for myself. Instead, I grab my dance clothes and walk down to the campus dance studio, which sits empty for the summer months. I stand in the silent studio, thinking back to the hours and hours I spent in here over the past year, learning the basics of jazz, ballet, and modern dance from two stellar teachers, Julie Strandberg and Gary Miller.

Julie and Gary changed the way I think and the way I use my body. They're equally responsible for the fact that I now carry myself erect, shoulders back; that my legs are streamlined and muscled, and can kick up to my nose; and that my body can bend and turn with precision and grace.

Gary, even taller than I, insisted I stop hiding in the back row and stand in the very front of the class so I could see myself in the mirrors. "Take up your space, girl!" he'd say, whacking me between the shoulder blades so I'd stand straight, "Your height is beautiful!"

Julie, who'd been my choreographer in Man of La Mancha, pushed me to come to class especially when I was struggling. She was right to do so. After a while, the nickel dropped, and my body just got it. "Well, look at you," I remember Julie saying, watching me happily and easily do fouettes across the studio floor. "You've actually turned into a dancer!"

Now I am addicted to the warm-up routines that began Julie's classes and do them daily. Today I have permission from Julie to use the studio to do those warm-ups, and it feels like I've won the lottery. No other bodies to potentially collide with. All the room in the world to extend my long legs and arms. No one blocking my view of myself in the mirror. It's dance heaven.

I click on the fluorescent lights, slip a copy of Pachelbel's Canon in D Major into the cassette player, and begin my warm-up routine. It's just me, the music, the wooden floor under my feet, the mirrors reflecting my body bending, folding, rolling, and unrolling. I feel my body un-kink, unwind, center, and settle. Done with the warm-up, I slip in another one of Julie's tapes, a contemporary instrumental, rhythmic and melodic. My body begins to follow the music, seeing where it leads, feeling where it takes me. I throw myself into the thicket of notes and rhythm, my long limbs lashing the air, my legs leaping and bounding with a will of their own across the yielding, empty floor. In that moment, nothing, absolutely nothing, seems out of my reach. I am spirit and flow personified, both dancer and dance. My body pulses with heat and happiness. The girl in the mirror lifts her face, suffused with power, passion, and grace. And all, all, is possible.

A young man with a backpack pauses outside the plate glass, watching. I am too engrossed to care.

For one brief moment, I don't give a damn who's watching or what they think.

*For one brief moment, I have both feet in—nothing wishy-washy about
this dance.*

For one, brief moment, I am truly me—sweaty, messy, magnificent.

For one brief moment, I know—truly know—I can do anything.

It will take me years to recover that feeling.

TWO FEET OUT

The feeling that within the happy rounds of play rehearsal, performances,
and communion with my actor pals—and epitomized by my solo dance
session—I had found my place lasted as long as the summer theatre season.
When the curtain went down on the last performance of the last play, I was
at a complete loss. Other fellow company members were excited about
their plans to go to graduate school in theatre, or to New York or Los Angeles
to try their hand at a professional career. But I had made no such plans and
was once again mired in fear, frozen by indecision. The lease was up on my
apartment, and there seemed to be only one option available: Returning
to my parents' home, to my little bedroom and to a life that seemed very,
very small. And so, memories of my transcendent summer already fading,
I threw my stage makeup, my scripts, and my jeans into my now worn
blue suitcases, shouldered my guitar, and went back, once again, to the
safety of the basement.

Once ensconced at my parents' house, I continued my pattern of flip-flop-
ping between possibilities. Should I go to New York? L.A.? Denver, where
my on-again, off-again college boyfriend had moved to go to law school?
Continuing my, by now, established pattern of indecision, I vacillated for
four, interminable months, much to my—and no doubt my parents—dismay
and general annoyance.

The double messages I got from my parents didn't help the situation: On
one hand, they (my mom especially) gave grudging lip service to the idea of

my permanently leaving the nest and finding work as an actress outside the Boston area. On the other hand, they strongly suggested I look for legitimate work (meaning anything but acting) in the Boston area. To make it harder for me to leave, they offered to buy me a queen size bed, as well as a new car for me to drive to what they hoped was the job I'd presumably find within commuting distance. I happily accepted the queen bed, tired of cramming my extra long body into the twin bed of my childhood; but I flatly refused the car. Intuitively, I knew that committing to the car meant committing to being a good little Greek girl par excellence, and living with my parents forever and ever, or at least until Prince Charming came along and swept me away to his swanky condo. Considering the new wings I'd sprung at Brown (I had been, after all, the chick singer in a band, and practically living with my boyfriend— behind my parents' backs, of course), this did not seem like a viable alterna- tive. And as married to being in limbo as I seemed to be, I knew on a deeper level that I didn't want to stay in the proverbial basement forever. Danged if that little voice inside kept piping up, "Could be more... you could sing for the world." If only I wasn't scared out of my mind to make a break for it.

It was the Macy's New Year's Day parade that kicked me into gear. Specifi- cally, it was seeing my very talented Brown University theatre colleague Scott Burkholder dressed as a pirate and frolicking with his cast mates on a float representing the Broadway show, *The Pirates of Penzance*, that made me sit up and think *What the hell am I doing?* I got serious cosmic goosebumps when I saw Scott, thinking *If Scott Burkholder can go to New York and get cast in a Broadway show within four months of graduation then I can too!*

So much to my parents' surprise and trepidation (not to mention my own), I bought a one-way train ticket to the Big Apple to seek my fame and fortune as an actress and singer.

POINTS TO PONDER

Many people choose to live their lives like they dance the Hokey Pokey— with one foot in and one foot out. On one hand they're yearning to make a change, a difference, an impact, or a stand. On the other hand, they refrain from taking the focused action that could bring their dreams, desires, and needs to fulfillment. Loathe to commit to one thing or another, they choose not to choose, and so they choose a kind of limbo by default.

This is especially true of women, who, according to a study by Anna Fels in the *Harvard Review*, tend to consider, then repeatedly reconsider an interest and often abandon it. They are quick to back off of their dreams and quick to apologize for their ambition (a dirty word for many females).[4]

I can attest to this. Many of my female coaching clients are stuck to and saddled with relationships that shrink their spirits, jobs they hate, or extra pounds that weigh down any good feelings they have about themselves. They're married to beliefs or attitudes that keep them stuck in neutral, pinioned to misery and gloom. Though they know they can and should take action to make change, and are even aware of the steps they need to take, they don't believe they are worthy of taking the steps to affect the change they so badly need. And so they stay exactly where they are—in limbo. They dream of being a novelist but never put pen to paper. They talk about going back to school but leave the application, unfilled, in the bottom drawer. They research the steps towards filing for divorce, but never take action to file the paperwork.

Maybe it's safer not to try. But are you really here to play it safe? Where, I ask, is playing it safe getting you?

This tendency to play it safe, to having one foot in and one foot out, often occurs in the way people handle and deliver their speeches, presentations, and communications. Refusing to make strong, bold choices, they begin and end their presentations with a whimper, meander with no direction throughout the body of the speech, and surrender to being utterly wishy-washy. Limbo, yet again.

Mark my words: When you choose limbo, with one foot in and one foot out of the basement, you never get anywhere. Which adds up to heartbreak, frustration, regret, and bitterness.

WELCOME TO BITTERTOWN

As the old saying goes, bitterness consumes the vessel that contains it. Bitter people tend to hang together, killing time, killing dreams, in a place I like to call Bittertown, the ultimate limbo. In Bittertown, the sign on the coffee-house reads: "Welcome to Bittertown, where the coffee is black and it burns you going down." In Bittertown, the streets are dim and dirty and littered with almosts, could-have-beens, and never-weres—the evidence of broken, unfinished, and unfulfilled lives.

We hang, shoulder-hunched, with our Bittertown comrades and kick the dust, bemoaning the fate that has doomed us to a dead-end life in a dead-end burg. We raise our fists to the heavens and blame everything and everyone for holding us back, holding us down, or keeping us from whatever we think we should be or have. We talk with rancor and envy about people we know who live on the outskirts of Bittertown, where the sun—and good fortune—always seems to shine on them.

Hooked to our martyred gloom, we shuffle by the dark and dingy storefronts, avoiding our shifting reflections in the windows because if we stop to really examine ourselves in the grimy glass, we would see, clearly and shockingly, that our choices brought us to the hopeless, aimless streets of Bittertown. The darkness and desolation are more comfortable for us to bear than the light of hope, joy, and abundance that shines and beckons on the periphery of Bittertown. And so we stay, attached to our pain, shame, and misery, unwilling to risk leaving what we know for the mystery of what lies outside.

If Bittertown sounds like where you're living, it's time for a new address. But only if you are willing to uproot and set off for a new environment, a new perspective, a new reality.

Stay in Bittertown, and languish in limbo.

Leave Bittertown, and leap with gusto and commitment into your life.

You have a choice. Which will it be?

SAY "AAA"

On a separate piece of paper, answer the following questions and complete the suggested exercises:

ATTITUDE

• What is your general attitude about staying in limbo? What fears or negative beliefs keep you from moving forward towards what you say you want to complete or accomplish?

• What affirmation can you create, repeat, and embrace to help you move through and out of a state of limbo (e.g., "I am willing to take the steps to move me forward.")?

ACTION

1. Where you do stand on taking a stand—for yourself, for your dreams, for your needs, and desires?

2. How willing are you to move out of what is comfortable for you for the sake of your dream, your desire, or the song in you?

3. What projects have you started and not finished? How does finishing—or even the idea of finishing—a project make you feel?

4. Imagine that you are on your deathbed. Looking back on your life, what project, dream, or desire will you have wished you had completed or attained during your lifetime? Write it down.

5. What *one* action step are you willing to take this week to encourage yourself to break free from being in limbo around a specific dream or project?

ACCOUNTABILITY

What will you do/what system of accountability will you put into place to help yourself complete this week's action step? Write it down.

CHAPTER FIVE

The Gift of Obstacles

"And the wind, it tried to blow her down,
The rain, to knock her flat,
And the bugs, they bit and tortured her
While the poppies turned their backs."
—ELENI KELAKOS, "THE TALLEST POPPY" FROM *TO THE BONE*

CLIMBING THE MOUNTAIN

I fell helplessly, completely in love with every fabulous, festering, fecund part of the Big Apple. The labyrinth of the subway system was mesmerizing, even when I got on the wrong train and wound up in a shifty part of Harlem at midnight. Even the hellhole that was then Times Square was entrancing— a heady mix of Broadway theatres, dance studios, audition halls, and triple X-rated peep shows.

For three months, I stayed with my exceedingly generous cousins at their very lovely Park Avenue apartment. But then, eager to feel and know the real New York, I lived in a succession of tiny apartments, awkwardly shared with strangers, from East Fourteenth Street to the Upper West Side (where I discovered I felt most at home). I finally lucked out and landed a small but lovely studio apartment of my very own on Seventy-second Street in a secure doorman building. My one window overlooked Broadway—and, more specifically, a little triangle of dirt and grass called Needle Park, so named because of its history as a haven for junkies and dope dealers. This tidbit of information was one I chose not to share with my parents.

In fact, there was a considerable amount of information I did not share with my parents, especially during my first few months in the city, when I seemed to attract every weirdo known to man. Like the flim-flam producer ("I know everybody! I can make you a star!") who tried to run his hand up my skirt at an interview. I knew enough to slap his hand away, and race past the junkies in the hallway of his sleazy office building to the relative safety of Forty-second Street. Or the truly underhanded skank of a voice-over producer who tried to convince me to record voice-over copy while using a rectal thermometer (yes, that's what I said: a rectal thermometer) because "a warm body produces better sound." I laughed in his face, shoved his smarmy chest, and ran out of his cushy office onto Madison Avenue, where, even in the throng of Friday rush hour pedestrians, I felt slimed, alone, and scared.

Still, I didn't let the weirdoes get to me. Sure, New York was jarring, dirty, and dangerous. Sure, there were predators lurking. But in my glazed-over haze of joy at actually being there, all I could think was so what? The pluses way outweighed the minuses—at least at this early point.

Besides, Professor Barnhill had been right in his verbal assessment of me delivered before I graduated from Brown:

"You've got a good head on your shoulders, Eleni. Stay grounded, and you'll be ok." He was right. I learned quickly who to avoid and who to trust, and soon was rarely, if ever, led astray by questionable characters promising fame and fortune.

I leaped full-tilt into my new life, earnestly learning how to be a professional actress and singer—the daily nuts and bolts of which I had not been taught in my Ivy League college. The very first thing I did was adopt the stage name

Eleni Markel, which was a combination of my middle name, Maria, and my last name, Kelakos. This was, interestingly enough, my dad's suggestion. He was worried my Greek name might hold me back—he'd lost some crucial job promotions because of his ethnic background and didn't wish the same for me. I never got used to my new name and felt like a fraud anytime anyone used it. I took my given name back about six months into the experiment, though I still have evidence of my temporary insanity by way of a playbill listing me as Eleni Markel from a children's production of *Cinderella* at the Penny Bridge Players in Brooklyn (I played an ugly stepsister). At the time, I didn't realize that reclaiming my real name was one of many steps I would eventually take in an effort to claim and embrace who I really was.

Following advice from other actors I quizzed, I had new headshots taken, printed up a resume, took jazz and ballet dance classes alongside real (and highly intimidating) Broadway dancers, found cheap pianists with whom I could practice my audition music, and did vocal warm ups every single day. I spent a vast amount of time learning the grid of the New York City streets so I could find the casting agencies and talent agencies listed in my trusty guide, the *Ross Reports* (called *Call Sheets* magazine, at the time of this writing), and drop off my photo and resume for their consideration. I learned to read *Drama-Logue* and *Back Stage* magazines, the theatre rags that listed audition dates and times, and began to attend non-union auditions, beginning to measure myself up against the talent at large. It was a scary and fabulous time. I could barely sleep at night, filled as I was with the light of possibility. Poems and prose in support of my art and my life force tumbled out of me at 2:00 or 3:00 a.m.

Like this, to a lover:
If you love me, and have the eyes that know the fire of a dreamer's soul, let me be free and full of my art... Be my lover and my deepest partner, but also let me mate with my art. I want so much to be consumed by it... I have been so careful, so far, so afraid to break, so afraid to fall. But, after all, this is why we are here: to risk all for greater things...to sing and soar.

Or this fervent oath:
I am committing myself to an art
that is greater than myself
but needs me as its vehicle.
This is my oath, my bond:
I swear, by my breath, in the humblest manner I bow to it.
I run to cherish it into being.
As of this moment,
I give myself over to this fire.

or this poem:
I lie
In the dense dark
Lit like a heat lamp
My blood, my bones, my skin glow
Hot.
From the inside out
I flame,
My soul sparks
Its back
Arcing like a black bear's.
Awake,
After sleeping long,
Winter is gone
In my soul, Spring.
A river dances
Vital, engorged, promising,
Power renewed,
Power affirmed.
My body whirs
Crackling life.

I lie
Bright
Fill the night.

I had never felt more alive. Every gritty inch of Manhattan seemed ready to deliver a new experience, a new possibility, or a new and exciting acquaintance. One autumn afternoon I was examining fruit at a Korean market on the upper West Side. Out of absolutely nowhere, I was accosted by a tall, elderly man with a white goatee, a plaid kilt, and a well-worn walking stick. His mighty, booming voice practically knocked the apple out my hand. "Who is this fantastic creature before me?" he bellowed, pointing his walking stick in my direction. Once I'd found my voice and introduced myself, I discovered I was talking to none other than Ed McCurdy, poet, singer, and the composer of the sixties' ode to peace, "Last Night I Had the Strangest Dream," a song I remembered from my trusty *Folk Song Handbook*.

Ed took me to a nearby coffee shop, recited snippets of his ribald, x-rated poetry in a voice loud enough to make the old ladies five booths away blush, and adopted me on the spot. A consummate creative artist, Ed wholly believed in making art for the sake of art. And he believed in me.

Soon after we met, Ed took me down to Folk City—a famous 1960's Mecca for singer-songwriters like Bob Dylan, Janis Ian, and Tom Paxton—where he emceed the weekly open mic, or hootenanny. At Ed's insistence, I stepped onto the rickety stage, shouldered my guitar and belted out the union anthem, "Joe Hill," a song I'd learned from an album by Joan Baez. Ed was very pleased with my performance, proclaiming me the genuine article. He offered me a nugget of advice, "It's better to be an artist, who works part time to support her art, than someone who works full time and shifts her art to the back burner. Be true to your muse!"

The more I considered Ed's advice, the more I wanted to heed it. I certainly did not want my art—the song in me, literally and figuratively—to get relegated to the back burner, or to the basement, the way my mom's did. And so I doubled my efforts to help the New York performing establishment realize that Eleni had arrived.

At first, I auditioned for singing jobs, easily nabbing steady gigs at cabaret rooms like The Horn of Plenty, Don't Tell Mama's, and The Green Street

Café in Soho. I put together an hour or so of show and pop tunes, put on a pretty dress, and sang to rooms full of diners, drinkers, and a growing mailing list of enthusiastic new fans. At one venue, I was regularly paid thirty-five whole dollars a show, in cash, and fed dinner. I did three shows a night: At 10:00 p.m., midnight, and 2:00 a.m. I loved being a part of New York City's neon-lit nightlife, belting out songs in the kinds of smoky, downtown clubs I'd only ever seen in movies.

But merely singing wasn't enough. The lure of Broadway was too great. I wanted so much to find my place on the Great White Way, or anywhere near it, for that matter. So I answered a call to audition for a compelling sounding production at the Lower East Side's famed avant-garde theatre, La Mama E.T.C. Called *The Plagues for Our Times*, this all sung, fully staged, a cappella musical oratorio for twenty voices was written by Eve Merriam and Tom O'Horgan. Tom, who was also directing, had been, I discovered, the director of the original Broadway productions of *Hair* and *Jesus Christ, Superstar*. Visionary and iconoclastic, Tom "got" me immediately, loving what he called "the basso profundo" quality of my voice. He also insisted I looked like the statue of a Cretan goddess with bare breasts and snakes in her hands that was one of his prized possessions. He called me his Greek Goddess and promptly cast me, much to my utter joy. I loved Tom, and trusted him immensely. He was very much like the Pied Piper, remarkably able to gently guide twenty young actors towards fulfilling his rather ambitious vision.

In this, my first foray into real, gritty, New York experimental fringe theatre, I wore a transparent black lace body suit, over a nude thong, black boots, and an earnest, intense expression. I assure you, my father, whose Parkinson's was, by now, keeping him house bound, glued to his TV chair, did not see me in this get-up. But my first agent, Fred Gorman, did, and for years, he never let me forget it.

I met Fred when he responded to an invitation to *The Plagues* that I'd sent to him—and a handful of other agencies—along with my photo, my resume, and a rather brash cover letter that began (in big letters):

"ELENI KELAKOS
I am UNIQUE as my name…"

When I visited Fred at his office for the very first time, he yelled, "it's Uni-cue!" I was baffled. Then he pointed to the wall behind him, where he had posted my picture and cover letter. "That's what we call you around here," he said, tapping the word "unique" with his finger, "Uni-cue."

My involvement with Fred Gorman netted me my very first job as a union card carrying professional actor. Fred called me out of the blue to audition at the last minute for The Guthrie Theatre's first foray into musical theatre—dual productions of *The Threepenny Opera* and *Guys and Dolls*. I had no idea that the Guthrie Theatre, located in Minneapolis, Minnesota, was the most prestigious regional theatre in the United States. Nor did I know that Liviu Ciulei, the director of the Guthrie and of *The Threepenny Opera*, was equally renowned. All I knew was they were looking for six-foot tall women, and that I had less than one hour to warm up my voice, get dressed, and get to the Minskoff rehearsal studios in midtown Manhattan, where auditions were being held.

The rest, as they say, is history. Though I was there simply to audition for the small part of a prostitute in Jenny Diver's whorehouse (a "speaking slut," as Fred termed it), Mr. Ciulei took a shine to me. He pulled me out of the pack of women auditioning, and, right then and there, had me learn and perform a song and a scene from the show. I didn't even have time to get nervous.

When Fred called to say I'd been cast in *The Threepenny Opera* not only as one of the whores, but as the understudy to both female leads, Polly and Lucy, he was as shocked as I. This was phenomenal, particularly since it would mean I was required to get my Actors Equity Association union card. Which meant I could finally, legitimately audition for Broadway shows. I was over the moon!

I flew to Minneapolis where I settled into a small apartment near the Guthrie and, for the first time in my adult life, became a real working actor—meaning I drew a salary large enough to live on. I woke up every day waiting for the bubble to burst. It didn't. I loved the uber-discipline of Liviu's rehearsals. I loved the fact that all I had to do was eat, live, and sleep theatre. And I dearly loved the cast mates with whom I'd spend three months of my life. If that was not enough, when the leading actress playing Polly Peachum got sick, I had the opportunity to go on in her place for two performances—both times at the nail-biting last minute. Fortunately for me I was absolutely ready. I'd spent hours beyond the required understudy rehearsals familiarizing myself with the role of Polly, just in case. So when I got my time in the spotlight, I was so ready that a visiting New York director thought I was the Julliard-trained actress originally cast in the part instead of the understudy. Score!

After my first stint as Polly Peachum, Barbara Andres, a beautiful, warm, caring woman and the fabulous actress playing Jenny Diver, walked me back to my apartment. She pulled me to a stop under a streetlight and told me, with certainly, that I was destined to do big things. "You're really talented and really capable," she said. "You're the kind of person that good things happen to, which might make other people envious of you."

I listened carefully—this was, after all, a woman with many years of top-of-the-line professional theatre experience. "There is no doubt in my mind that you'll do Broadway," she said. *From her lips to God's ears*, I thought, on cloud nine and still rising.

I returned to New York with a prestigious regional theatre acting credit on my resume, and my Actor's Equity card in my wallet, convinced that, as Barbara Andres had reassured me, it would be a hop, skip, and a jump to my Broadway debut.

Boy, was I wrong.

DOWN, DOWN THE SLIPPERY SLOPE

I'm standing in the wings of Broadway's Broadhust Theatre, fishnetted knees knocking, next in line to audition for the part of Claudia in the musical Nine. My heart is skipping like a scratched CD: All these beautiful actresses. They seem so—so—professional, so poised and prepared, warming up their stunning voices with practiced vocal exercises, putting finishing touches on their perfectly made-up faces.

Watching tight-knit groups of girls chat conspiratorially, I feel like I'm back in junior high school, the awkward one, out on the fringe. Everything about me feels wrong: The filmy, silver-flecked black chiffon scarf that keeps slipping from my shoulders, the mini dress and spike heels that make me look and feel like a somber, unsteady drag queen. Moe and Shmoe, the little judgers in my head, are having a field day. "You don't belong here!" they hiss. "Those other women are real actors. You're a fraud."

"Elahhnee Kolaykuss."

The scrawny little man who has butchered my name holds a clipboard and points me in the direction of the stage.

"You're up," he says.

THUNK! My heart drops into my stomach.

The stage is slippery and at a slight angle, designed for better viewing of the dance numbers, but treacherous for walking in high heels. I clatter out like an uncertain gazelle, blinking in the sudden wash of lights. A disembodied voice— the casting director? the producer?—leaps at me from the thick, foreboding darkness beyond the lip of the stage. "Please take your sheet music to the pianist and start when you're ready."

I turn and see a bored-looking fellow idling on the keys of a shiny grand piano about a mile away across the slick stage. Carefully, I make my way to him, praying not to slip and fall on my barely-clothed butt. With a grunt, he snatches my music—"I'll Be Seeing You," a ballad from the 1930's—and lays it on the piano. He reels off the musical introduction. Am I ready? Who the heck knows? I turn to face the black hole that is the audience and begin to sing.

The voice that comes out of my mouth feels disembodied, curiously not my own. It's as if I'm watching and listening to myself from above, a strange, disquieting sensation—one that I'll be able to describe in vivid detail to the coaching clients who will, thirty years later, come to me for help in tackling their own performance anxiety. My body is frozen from the neck down, a wooden, stilted object. All those moments on all those stages, starring in plays, strutting confidently in front of a band, and I suddenly don't know who I am or what I'm doing. So this is what it feels like to be on a Broadway stage, *my mind whispers. The thought fades as quickly as it comes. My lips mouth the words of the song, but I am not in control.*

I near the last lap of the song in what can only be described as a state of jittery panic. As I round the bend towards the final note, a shrill, wavering sound fills my ears. Oh my God, that sound is me! It's my own voice, skewering a note so badly, punting it so far off course that it has probably landed in a stinking heap in New Jersey!

The piano tinkles to a standstill. Not a peep from the Powers That Be out in the pitch black house. Finally, two words, flung dispassionately from the darkness: "Thank you." I wobble and weave my way off the stage, face red, heart stuttering. I have never sung so badly in my life.

As I exit the dusty theatre, and stumble, round-shouldered, back to my apartment, I don't congratulate myself on getting through my first, harrowing Broadway audition, chalking it up to experience. Oh, no. Instead, I focus on how I failed; how I didn't come through; how blatantly imperfect I am. I beat myself into an emotional pulp. And then, behind the closed doors of my little apartment, overwhelmed with anxiety and self-loathing, I practice a newfound and disturbing ritual: I shove whatever food I can grab into my mouth—cereal, peanuts, pickles, cookies—pushing my anxiety down with every mouthful, intent on filling a void that seems endlessly, impossibly deep. Finally, when there is no food left, and I'm so full, so disgusted with myself that I can't stand it anymore, I indulge in the second, most damning part of my secret ritual: I walk in a daze to the bathroom, plunk my mini-skirted behind onto the tiled floor, poke my finger towards the back of my throat, and make myself puke. This is my sacred rite, the ritual of the good girl, the perfect girl, the straight-A student pleaser who has somehow failed just by being human. Look at Canton's gift to Broadway now.

I am the perfect, bulimic prototype. Only, since it's 1982, and no one is talking about it yet, I don't know what bulimia is. Crying on the floor of my bathroom, staring into the unblinking eye of the dirty toilet, all I know is I am shame and disappointment personified, and if my boyfriend, my parents, my brother, my friends, my agent could see me now, they would probably disown me. And so, of course, I will not tell them. Ever. I am both master of and slave to the carefully constructed, cheery façade I've built to protect the world from what must surely be my unforgivably dark, anxious, hidden, and patently unlovable, nature.

In the morning, I lie to myself and swear I will never, ever do that again. And then, determined, smiling, I leap out into the world towards yet another audition—"Pick me! Pick me!"—and yet another rejection.

The cycle is vicious. The cycle is magnetic. And I am fully, inexorably, in its grasp.

STILL FURTHER DOWN THE SLIPPERY SLOPE

Desperate to get cast, struggling with an eating disorder, juggling subsistence jobs (temp work, waitressing, playing Spider Woman in shopping malls), I did something really quite confounding: I fell in love and got married. Instead of focusing on my work, finding a great therapist, and tackling my demons, I grabbed onto a handsome, charming life preserver by the name of Marcus. A successful actor, eight years my senior, Marcus was everything I wanted to be—a working actor who seemed to book every audition he went on.

I, on the other hand, was turning into what I teasingly called "The Callback Queen"—a term that, after a year of coming within a hair's breadth of acting roles I desperately wanted, wasn't funny anymore. In my journal, I wrote:

Nobody told me I'd have to scrape my way to the top.
Every inch seems a mile.
Every yes holds the shadows of a thousand no's.
I guess that's how it goes.

It's not that directors and producers weren't interested. They were, at least initially: I was called back time and time again for interesting, challenging productions—callbacks that involved singing, dancing, acting, interpretive movement to poetry, and wild improvisations with a skeleton puppet as tall as me. I knocked myself out at these auditions, but the role would invariably go to someone else. And usually someone, well, shorter.

"We need someone exactly like you, only five-foot-four," a casting director once told me, with genuine regret, after a particularly good audition. "You're wonderful. But the guy you'd be playing opposite would be up to your navel. It just won't work."

Another casting director, for a daytime soap, told me, flatly, "You're too tall for soaps. Period." Nothing I said or did could convince him otherwise.

It was infuriating. And confusing. After all, Marcus was almost six-foot-four, and his height sure wasn't stopping him. I started to get it: If you were a man, being tall was fine. Because it seemed that anyone with any power to give me an acting job in the New York theatre scene believed that men should be taller than women. Like Barbie and Ken dolls. Only I was more like Ken.

Day after day, month after month, I auditioned, getting more and more frustrated with every "No!" and every "Too tall." The more I was rejected, the more desperate I got. The more desperate I got, the more I was rejected.

The more I was rejected, the harder I tried to please. The more I tried to please, the less effective my auditions became. It was a terrible, vicious circle.

One horrible day, it all came to a head.

MISS THING

I'm at an audition for a prestigious talent agent I'll call Miss Thing. In my desperate and delusional state, I am convinced that even though I already have an agent, Fred, I need a new one to shake things up. Someone who is possibly tougher and shrewder. Someone like Miss Thing.

For the past month, I've been rehearsing a speech from a play that I'm convinced is going to wow Miss Thing to such a degree that she'll sign me on the spot and make me a star.

The receptionist tells me that despite my scheduled appointment, Miss Thing is on the phone and I'll have to wait. So, I sit in a chair, and I wait. And I wait. And I wait. The same way I waited for someone to ask me to dance back in junior high school.

I wait fifteen minutes. Thirty minutes. One hour and twenty minutes.

I am now united as one with the leather chair.

Finally, a door swings open, and Miss Thing waltzes in. No smile. No "I'm so sorry I kept you waiting." Nothing. She merely gestures for me to follow her into her office.

Then she scans my body, from my toes, up, up, up to the top of my head. Being that she is half my height, that takes an unbearably long time.

"You're not just tall," she says. "You're too tall."

Those are her very first words to me, "You're not just tall, you're too tall."

Like a balloon, I start to deflate.

PSHHHHHHHHHHHHHHHHT!

"Stand over there and do your monologue for me," she barks. "I don't have all day!"

I schlump into the corner and turn. Her face is a stone wall.

I open my mouth. The monologue I've been painstakingly rehearsing for the last thirty days falls from my lips like pieces of cold, wet clay.

Blah.
Blah blah blah.
Blah.
Blah blah.

No passion. No purpose. No Eleni-ness. No nothing.

When I'm done, there's a horrible silence in the room.

Finally, Miss Things speaks.

"Well," she says, "I've heard that speech many times before, and you brought absolutely nothing remarkable to it."

PSHHHHHHHHHHHHHHHHHHTtttttttttttttttt.

I shrink further.

"It doesn't matter," Miss Thing says, "because I'm not going to sign you. You know why? You're too tall and you're never going to work. You're never going to work." Then she turns away from me and reaches for her phone.

I'll repeat that: She turns away from me and reaches for her phone.

I stand there, and for a moment I think I'm done. This is it. I give up. I'm going back to the basement. I belong in the basement. I like the basement.

But there's that little nagging inner voice again, surprisingly loud, "Could be more! You could sing for the world!"

And I think Wait a minute, this is what I love! This is what I'm good at, this is what I know is right for me! *And suddenly, something snaps! Suddenly, I am on fire, hot little prickles crawl up my spine and the back of my head. I re-inflate in a big rush, I stand as tall I can be, look Miss Thing in the eye and I say,* "I have worked. And I'm going to work again, and again! And I don't need your help to do it!"

And I turn my back on her, and march out of her office.

I march out of her office!

In that moment, I choose to touch the sky.

And oh! Is that sweet.

BUT ON THE OTHER HAND

My elation was short lived. Because even though I reclaimed a little bit of myself when I chose to leave that office, I still had to face the fact that Miss Thing had been right.

She'd been *right*. Not about my being too tall—that was her opinion, and I didn't have to agree with it. She was right about the fact that my monologue stunk up the room.

And that wasn't her fault. It was mine. Because nobody can take away your power. Unless you let them.

This point is so important, I'm going to say it again. Nobody can take away your power. Unless you let them.

I *let* Miss Thing make me feel small. I *let* her intimidate me. I *let* myself shrink under her gaze. I *let* her stop me from showing her how great I really was. I betrayed myself. I'd come so close to giving up my dream, and my goal, and hiding my song in the basement. Forever.

SOUND FAMILIAR?

Have you ever done that? Have you given your power away to someone else just because you were intimidated by them, or you wanted to please them? Have you ever let someone else abuse you, mistreat you, or insult you, and then blamed them for how lousy you felt?

I want you to do me a favor. I want you to put this book down, just for a second, and hold out your hands in front of you, like you're cradling a flickering flame, like you're protecting something tender and precious and vulnerable. What I want you to see in your hand is the essence of your passion, your purpose, your potential, your uniqueness, your talents, dreams, and desires. See the song in you, the mission and purpose that fuels the work you do. Look at it, cradled in your hand, see and recognize its worth and value— your worth and value.

Now, on the count of three, I want you to clap your hands together. One! Two! Three!

That's how quickly the song in you can die. That's how quickly you can give it away. That's how quickly you can let someone, something, or even yourself, snuff it out. The song in you is indescribably precious. It's entirely up to you to protect it, to fuel it, and to keep it alive.

Because nobody can take away your power. Unless you let them.

STARING INTO THE ABYSS

I wish I could tell you that this realization made a vast difference in my downward spiral.

It did not.

I was too far gone at that point.

And while I was spiraling downward, Marcus was spiraling upwards, booking more and more work. Embarrassing as it is to admit, I was jealous, even rage-full.

The darkness of winter began to shut me in. The steam pipes hissed and rattled as I tossed and turned in bed, worrying, worrying, worrying. Nothing was going as planned. The golden girl, the perfect girl, the but-I-always-get-straight-A's-and-the-leads-in-plays girl was failing. I had never failed before. What would my parents think? How could I face them?

The doors continued to slam shut, one audition after another.

No. No. No.

Each no felt like a nail in the coffin of my acting career.

My grief, my anxiety ambushed me. I stuffed it down with food, keeping my binging and purging from my husband, folding my shame over myself like a dark cloak of doom.

The song in me got very, very small. Almost imperceptible.

And just when I thought things couldn't get much worse, they did.

WELCOME TO THE EDGE

At brunch at a neighborhood restaurant one morning, with Marcus and an old friend, I began to feel dizzy, unable to take a full breath, as if the space around my head and lungs was contracting. My feet and fingers jumped, tapped, twitched. My thoughts grew wild, outsized, tangled. My heart seemed to be pushing its way out of my chest, beat by deafening beat. Lurching out of my chair, I stammered an excuse and raced to the bathroom. In the restroom mirror, a wild-eyed, hyper-ventilating woman looked back at me. Who was this woman? Where was the smiling little diva girl with light in her eyes?

Back at the table, finally calmed, I said not a word about what I soon grew to realize had been a massive panic attack.

The following morning I woke up and discovered that New York City had morphed into an interconnected set of threatening, monstrous, and strangely beckoning rooftops, balconies, and terraces. Suddenly, I was afraid of the city. Afraid of the deck outside my bedroom window, and the six-floor drop at the end of it. Afraid I would walk out on to the deck and throw myself off the edge.

Because for the first time in my short life, I didn't see the point of living. If I couldn't be perfect, if I couldn't be "Canton's Gift to Broadway," if I couldn't prove my worth to my parents, to the people whose voices I had let overshadow my own, what right had I to live?

Little did I know that confronting that question would be the very thing that would save my sanity and my life.

....

POINTS TO PONDER

Obstacles. Life just wouldn't be life without them.

As you have no doubt discovered—and as I so painfully learned during my early years in New York City—our life paths, even when we're sure of them—

are not a straight shot from here to there. Because life is not a Disney movie. And our lives are more like obstacle courses.

It's like this: You start out on your path, giddy and hopeful, your passion and purpose nipping at your heels, prodding you forward towards your goal when BAM! Obstacles and challenges—Bills! Rejections! Illness! Tsunamis! Self-destructive thoughts!—leap out like linebackers, intent on dragging you down.

Take deciding to quit smoking, for example. As soon as you make the decision to never have another cigarette again, suddenly everyone around you is lighting up and offering you a drag. "C'mon," your smoking pals from work entreat, "at least just hang out with us on the back steps and keep us company." And you do. And then you think *I'll just have one puff, one tiny little puff.* And BAM! You're hooked again.

Obstacles and challenges are a gimme—a necessary and unavoidable part of our lives. When they're not coming at us from the outside, we're providing them ourselves from the inside by way of negative thoughts and attitudes that keep us small, scared, and stuck.

But here's kicker: I think obstacles are gifts in disguise.

I know what you're thinking. "Eleni, what wacky weed have you been smoking? Obstacles are *gifts*? Are you nuts?"

To that I say, "What's wrong with being a little nutty?"

And I stand by my statement: Obstacles are gifts. Because every time you run into one—thrown at you by outside forces or created by your own beliefs and attitudes—you get to ask yourself those all-important questions: "Will I choose to play small? Or will I choose to be all I can be and touch the sky? Will I choose to let this obstacle diminish my purpose, my passion, my dreams, desires, needs, abilities, talents, and goals? Or will I choose instead to figure a way through, up, and around it, so I can be all I can be?"

Because, as I will now mention for the fourth time, nobody can take away your power. Unless you let them. Nothing can take away your power. Unless you let it.

CHOOSING TO MINE THE SILVER LINING

Many of my fellow motivational speakers have turned catastrophic, life-changing events, obstacles, and challenges into opportunities to teach, serve, and uplift others. That includes brilliant and inspiring speakers like Jackie Pflug, (shot in the head by hijackers and left for dead on the airport tarmac); W. Mitchell (paralyzed and burned from head to toe from both a car accident AND a plane crash), and Paul Templer (attacked and maimed by an enraged hippopotamus). They have learned to mine the silver lining of their cloud of challenges to the great good fortune of the people whose lives they touch.

This is exactly what my client, Lauren Parrott, a radiant, charismatic woman in her late twenties, has done. Five days before her high school graduation, Lauren was diagnosed with multiple sclerosis (MS). At first, she felt kicked in the teeth and downright depressed. And she could very well have chosen to stay that way, slouched in the basement, keeping the song in her all to her-self. Instead, she decided to step out into the world and use her considerable gifts as a natural, ebullient communicator to help people understand MS and how it affects those diagnosed with it.

With a background in television, a knack for public speaking, and an infec-tious, uplifting personality, Lauren was born to be on a stage. And that's where you'll find her, lifting hearts and souls everywhere as a motivational speaker. Sharing her story, Lauren encourages the members of her audi-ence to be less judgmental and more supportive of people with disabilities. She also regularly records and posts videos about MS-related issues on her website (www.laurenparrot.com) giving people with MS, and the family and friends who love them, a platform for community, support, and information. As of this writing, Lauren has posted almost one hundred videos and has an active viewership. Lauren refuses to let the challenges of her diagnosis stop her in her tracks, preferring to see it as an opportunity to affect other people's lives for the better. In the face of a formidable obstacle, Lauren has clearly chosen to touch the sky.

Faced with even the greatest of challenges, you, like Lauren, have the power to choose what you think, what you believe, and what action you can take in the face of challenge. Every time you resist the urge to make the song in you smaller, you gain a degree of personal power, of grace, of self-respect that all the money in the world can't buy.

As you'll discover in the next chapter, that's what I learned as I looked off the edge of a six-story building, contemplating my fate.

SAY "AAA"
On a separate piece of paper, answer the following questions and complete the suggested exercises:

ATTITUDE
- What is your general attitude about obstacles and challenges? What do you tend to think, believe, or do when faced with an obstacle?

- What affirmation can you create, repeat, and embrace to maintain a more positive attitude towards obstacles (e.g., "I look for the lesson in every obstacle or challenge.")?

ACTION
1. List the top three obstacles or challenges you have experienced in your life so far. What useful life lessons or positive growth did you experience as a result of these obstacles?

2. What obstacles or challenges are you currently facing? What opportunities for growth and learning could they offer you?

3. On a large piece of paper, write out every obstacle and every fear
that is currently stopping you. Let the sentences fall on the page
in random patterns—vertical, horizontal, sideways—so that, all
together, they form a large, interconnected spider web. This is the
web of fear that is holding you back. Once you've dumped all of
your fear and all of your obstacles onto the paper, find a ritualistic
way to destroy it (Burn it? Rip into pieces?) and simply let it go.

4. What *one* action step are you willing to take this week to encourage yourself to see your obstacles as gifts or move up and around
a challenge?

ACCOUNTABILITY
What will you do/what system of accountability will you put into
place to help yourself complete this week's action step?

CHAPTER SIX

The Gift of Choice

"And if I want, I can lead the way,
I can make a choice, and claim this day.
And if I want I can lend a hand,
I can speak my mind and take a stand and
Hope begins with me..."
—ELENI KELAKOS, "HOPE BEGINS WITH ME" FROM *TOUCH THE SKY*

I sit upright in my rumpled bed, confused: *Why is the apartment blazing with light in the middle of the night? Didn't I turn the lights off before I went to bed?*

In spite of my pajama-clad body, I feel weightless, floaty. My attention turns to the light from the living room that reaches up the circular staircase like a lover's beckoning arms. I must follow that light and travel down the stairs, this is certain. And so, the energy that is my essence begins to rise and gather, building up steam and focus like an engine revving. Without effort, I leave my heavy body on the bed, picking up speed as I whip and snake down and around the coils of stairs, towards the pull of the living room. As I near the bottom of the stairs, a whooshing rush of disembodied self, my attention is pulled towards the sliding glass doors and the terrace beyond them. Though I know I locked them last night, the doors are now flung wide, inviting. And in the glow of the terrace light, I see it: The collection of bricks and mortar that forms the balcony; the balcony that delineates The Edge.

I realize it, and I accept it. I am hurtling towards The Edge,
The Edge that has held me in its trance for three anguished weeks. The Edge,
that, once breached, invites a six-floor drop to an unyielding concrete courtyard.
I have imagined this scene many times. But now, I am experiencing it.

The energy that I am picks up greater speed and purpose and races like a freight
train towards The Edge.

And as The Edge rushes towards me, I feel no fear. I know without a doubt that
whether I choose to stop before The Edge or fly over it, I—this whooshing,
purposeful, disembodied self—will be fine.

I have a choice. There is always a choice. And so I choose.

I come to a screeching halt in front of The Edge.

And then, I wake up.

I have always had dreams that feel as vivid as real life, but this one was like no
other. Almost thirty years later, I can still remember the depth, detail, and
feeling of the dream, as if it had just occurred. Was it a dream, an out-of-
body experience? I don't know, and it doesn't matter. What does matter is
that it changed me forever. I had gone to sleep, anxious, fearful, battling the
strange, obsessive desire to peer and possibly leap over the edge that had had
me in its grip for days. I woke up completely freed from the need to do so.
The dream was eerie, uncanny. And it saved my life.

Or, I should say, the choice I made to stay on the nearer side of the edge saved
my life. Because I was keenly aware that the choice was entirely up to me.

Now, I'm not saying that I was suddenly and miraculously recovered from
my underlying sense of despair and the feelings of low self-worth that had
spawned this obsession. I'm saying that my eyes had been opened to the possibility that it was my right—and my duty—to make choices on my own behalf,
for my own well-being. I also had the will to choose actions that would

benefit and not harm me. Of that I was now certain.

For someone who had spent a lifetime making choices on behalf of everyone else, this revelation was a game changer.

MAKE A CHOICE AND STICK WITH IT

The notion of making a choice and standing by it was not a new one for me. As an actor, I had been trained to understand the value of making strong choices and holding to them. The process of rehearsing a script and developing a character involves making a series of choices, one building on the last. Every acting teacher I had ever had emphasized the need to not only make a choice, but to make a bold choice. The bolder, stronger, and clearer the choice, the more defined your character and the more clear and accessible the material became for your audience and your fellow actors.

But, as is evident from my history of vacillation, I had never applied this concept to myself, my needs, and the song in me. It was time for a change. Since I had absolutely nothing to lose, and only myself to gain, I made a bold choice, a strong choice:

I called a therapist.

CHOOSING TO REACH OUT

The fact that I thumbed through the yellow pages and looked up "Therapists" was, in fact, more than bold. In my little world, it was a revolutionary act. I had, after all, been raised to believe that it was not seemly to ask for help— especially (gasp!) professional help. Engaging a therapist would imply that things were not as perfect as they appeared to be, not only within the confines of my head, but within the confines of the Kelakos clan. But I intuitively knew that, in order to survive and ultimately thrive, I needed help. I also knew I wasn't going to get it from my family. Sharing my dirty laundry with people outside the circle of my immediate family was just not done. But, then again, neither was sharing my dirty laundry with members of my immediate family.

When I timidly called my mother and told her I was having self-destructive thoughts, she very primly said, "Not *my* daughter," and that was the end of that conversation. I, of course, never mentioned it to my dad, not wanting to burden him on top of his progressive illness; and I never broached the subject with my brother, George, who, years later, chided me for it. And when it came to sharing my deepest fears with my husband, well, it was obvious to me that, while he cared about my mental and personal health, my condition was overwhelming to him, and it was easier for him to stay as removed from it as possible. Broken open as I was, I reflected poorly on him. Where had his happy, flawless "little one" (his term for me) gone? And how would that look to others?

So, I called a therapist, and started examining my underpinnings, kicking off what would be a life-long commitment to self-growth and self-exploration.

I also called three of my closest friends, Suzi, Claude, and Amy, and filled them in on what was going on. This, too, was a revolutionary act. After all, I would be revealing something bleak and ugly about myself—what if they turned away from me? If my family couldn't accept me for who I really was and what I was going through, how could my friends?

When I reached out to Suzi, Claude, and Amy, they reached back with love, acceptance, and rock-solid support. They also reached out with some relief, glad that I was finally willing to really show myself to them as I fully was, warts and all. In the process, I learned that there's the family we're born into and the family we create. And the latter is often more accepting and supportive than the former.

In retrospect, I realize I had intuitively taken one of the most important actions a person can take when struggling and overwhelmed: I'd chosen to reach out to others. And by making that choice, I discovered the simple truth that sharing my pain made it less burdensome.

CHOOSE YOUR THOUGHTS, CHOOSE YOUR WORDS

During this time, and on a day when I was really struggling, I coincidentally ran into an acquaintance named Laurie on the streets of Manhattan. She took one look at me and deduced that I was not in a good way. Grabbing my hand, she led me to her apartment, which was conveniently just around the corner. Once there, she switched off the phone, turned off the lights, pulled down the shades, and insisted I lie down on her couch with my eyes closed. Then she did something for which I will always be grateful. She turned on her cassette player and played self-help guru Louise Hay's morning affirmation tape. Louise's soothing voice affirmed that my thoughts weren't set in stone: I had the power to change them, and in so doing, I could shape and change my life. I grabbed onto Louise Hay's words as if they were little life preservers. Once her final, comforting words washed over me—"all is well... I love you"—I opened my eyes, sat up, and hugged Laurie with all of my heart.

The gift she gave me that day, by way of Louise Hay, was instrumental—not only for my immediate recovery, but for the impact it would have on both my personal life and my life's work. I had never before thought about the power of my thoughts or of the words I used that reflected those thoughts. I immediately bought Louise's book, *You Can Heal Your Life,* and read it cover to cover. I also bought a copy of her morning and evening affirmations tape, and committed to listening to it twice a day for an entire month. At the end of thirty days, I had internalized the essential, positive messages to such a degree that I knew I could never completely go back to the negative thoughts and beliefs that had kept me so small and scared. Taking Louise Hay's suggestions to heart, I began to create my own, positive, uplifting affirmations, and to speak them out loud. "I am willing to be all that I am!" "I am worthy and wonderful!" For the first time in my life, I used my words, and my voice, to give myself strength and succor.

THE JOY OF JOURNALING

I had kept a diary since I was fourteen years old, but now I wrote daily with a reinvigorated desire to voice my thoughts and to understand myself. My therapist encouraged it, calling it "journaling," which I thought sounded better than "diarying." I was glad that something I already loved doing was so good for me. Looking back at some of my writing, I realize I was not only helping myself back into my own life, but working out some of the central themes of the work I would wind up exploring with my coaching clients—themes of self-confidence, self-expression, and self-development—that are relevant, thirty years later, to this very chapter in this very book. Talk about cosmic clues.

Looking back at some of the journal entries from that time, it's apparent that I not only used my written words to work out my feelings, but also to bolster myself. My written words served as positive, uplifting affirmations, egging me on towards new, more life-affirming actions. They were, in fact, the written equivalent of the loud music my college roommate, Sue, often put on the stereo on Friday afternoon to get herself pumped up for the weekend. Sue, who was from New Jersey, blasted Bruce Springsteen, "The Boss," and called it her "Psych Music." My journal entries served the same purpose. Here are a few examples from December 1987 and January 1988:

"I am like nobody else... Sometimes I forget about how wonderful that is.... The idea is not to want to be like (anybody) else... or to put myself down for being so Eleni. The idea is to celebrate my uniqueness and to explore it as fully as possible. I need to claim my space, define myself and my needs and capabilities, and go for it."

* * * * * * *

"I choose to live, for myself first... I choose to be on this earth to let my vitality sing through me..."

* * * * * * *

"...even world leaders have moments of despair and depression. I am not perfect, I am simply me. Human and vulnerable and special in my own way."

* * * * * * *

"I must seek stability and a center IN ME."

* * * * * * *

"Facing the fear, the roof (The Edge) head-on, as I did, saying no aloud to this demon, asking myself, brutally, 'is THIS what you want?' and realizing that, in truth, what I want is to LIVE, but fully, enriched, not this half-life, caught in my own fears, was a great step."

* * * * * * *

"Feel like I'm teetering between giving up my power completely and claiming my power completely. My deep inner voice says 'move towards claiming your power, it will feel best, it is the best for you'.... it feels better to get this stuff OUT of me and on paper."

* * * * * * *

"...I woke up very anxious again... took me a while to shake it, but I did... music helped, as did simply doing physical things. I HAVE A CHOICE IN THE MAT-TER! I have the choice of either giving up my reins completely, or taking them up into my own hands and steering my life...I choose to pull myself out of and above the muck and the mire... so screw YOU doom and gloom! I choose joy and life, and you can go to hell!"

* * * * * * *

Committed to choosing new, more useful thoughts and actions and to allowing myself to fully take up the space I was born to inhabit, I wrote the following list of New Year's resolutions.

New Year's Resolutions, 1988

I resolve to take a total and active responsibility for my life, shaping and guiding
*   it in positive and fulfilling directions.*
I resolve to treat myself with love, patience, and respect.
I resolve to claim my full power, honoring my talents, energies, and abilities.
I resolve to reach out of myself more to friends and family, especially when I am
*   feeling low.*
I resolve to spend time daily, meditating and making positive affirmations.
I resolve to allow myself not to have to be perfect.

By choosing to reach out for help, embrace new thoughts and beliefs, use positive affirmations to bolster my newly minted sense of self, and express myself through written words, I had began to change my life and to re-connect to my passion and purpose. In the face of some enormous challenges, I had embraced the power of choice: Instead of choosing to make myself smaller, I was, more often than not, choosing to touch the sky.

....

POINTS TO PONDER

Nowhere do I see the principles of the gift of choice reflected more than in my presentation skills coaching or life coaching work.

Time and time again, I am approached for presentation skills coaching by brilliant, accomplished, capable clients who are convinced they are, among other things, incorrigibly boring, destined to forever feel performance anxiety, or at risk of being found out for the frauds they think they are.

Feeling like a fraud, unworthy of the accolades or respect you have rightfully earned, is so prevalent, that it's even been given a term—The Impostor Syndrome. In fact, the last time I Googled the words "Impostor Syndrome," there were over 328,000 results. (Note: If you'd like to learn more about this, take a look at Dr. Valerie Young's book *The Secret Thoughts of Successful Women: Why Capable People Suffer from the Impostor Syndrome and How to Thrive in Spite of It.*)

When clients first come to me for life or career coaching, they are convinced they're destined to stay forever stuck where they are—in jobs they hate, in relationships that are diminishing them—voiceless, joyless, and self-less. The same holds true for my presentation skills coaching clients, who are sure they will always be afraid to speak in public or never be able to bring color, humor, or humanity to their presentations. It's my job to gently help them under-stand that—most of the time—the only thing that's holding them back from making changes that will open them up to new, more fulfilling experiences as speakers and as people, is them. Or, more specifically, the thoughts they are choosing to think and the actions they are choosing to take based on those thoughts.

Early on in the coaching process, I roll up my sleeves and do what I call discovery work. Through a series of questions and creative exercises, I help my clients pinpoint the limiting thoughts and beliefs they are choosing to think and believe that are holding them back, and then I work with them to create and implement new, more useful and supportive thoughts and beliefs that can move them forward. It's a process that takes time and patience. But, as I am always saying to my clients, old habits die hard—and they die only when you choose to kill them and replace them with new, more productive habits. Since it takes X amount of time to acquire the old habits, thoughts, and beliefs that have been tripping you up, it stands to reason that it will take X amount of time to replace them with new ones.

The operative word in this process is *choice*. In order to make a change, you first have to choose to want to make a change. And then, of course, you have to choose to take action.

MOE AND SCHMOE

I'm confident in saying there isn't a person alive who hasn't experienced the disconcerting, self-defeating, self-pummeling administered by their personal inner gremlins... You know, those little inner judges that sound suspiciously like negative Nellie, the aunt who always invoked doom and gloom, or shaming Stan, the eighth grade algebra teacher who always made you feel you'd never amount to anything, no matter how hard you tried. I like to call these little personal naysayers Moe and Schmoe. I imagine them perching on my shoulders, hissing bile into my ears, two ugly, gnome-like little beings dedicated to my undoing. Moe and Schmoe come out swinging when I am feeling most vulnerable—waiting to go on stage to present to a tough audience, fielding a verbal challenge by a resistant coaching client, auditioning for a role that could potentially change my life—and I have had to learn to silence them. Or at least put them in their place.

The process is fairly simple: Step one is recognizing that your inner judgers exist (hence, naming them). Step two is taking note of what they tend to say (e.g., "You are a talentless lout, and no one is going to take you seriously."). Step three is reworking the negative statement into a written affirmation that is infinitely more useful, hopeful, and pleasing (e.g., "I am uniquely talented and gifted, and because I take myself seriously, others do too!"). Step four (perhaps the most important step) is choosing to internalize the new thoughts and beliefs by committing to work with them daily.

I encourage my clients to speak their new affirmations out loud as often as possible. I even suggest they go so far as to put them all together into a document I call a personal manifesto, which we record for them to listen to in the morning before they start their day, in the evening before they fall asleep, and any time they need a boost to prepare to perform under pressure.

The more my clients allow themselves to embrace their new thoughts and beliefs, the less power Moe and Schmoe have over them, and the easier it is for them to begin to take steps forward, out of the muck and the mire. Repetition is key. That's because the subconscious mind (where Moe and Schmoe live) is, according to research presented in a lecture I attended by brain scientist, Dr. Bruce Lipton, one hundred times more powerful than the conscious mind. Remarkably, the subconscious mind is in charge 95 percent of the time.[5]

Examples of the power of your subconscious mind abound. Once, after facilitating a half-day training in Lansing, Michigan, an hour and a half from my home, I hopped into my Toyota Prius, turned on "Prissy," the navigation system, and headed for the freeway. My phone rang just as I was turning onto the freeway entrance. I answered it (I know, I know, I was driving, and I shouldn't have). For the next twenty minutes, I drove and talked, talked and drove. All the while, Prissy was barking her orders at me ("take a left, stay in the right lane," etc.). I ignored her completely, however, so engrossed was I in my conversation. Fifteen miles later, I suddenly popped back into the present moment and realized two things: (1) Prissy was yelling at me to "make a legal U turn" and go back in the other direction, and (2) the nearest street sign told me I was going back into Lansing, not away from it. Here's what was really scary: For twenty minutes, I had essentially been driving my car unconsciously—switching lanes, avoiding other cars, speeding up, or slowing down without even realizing it. That's how powerful our subconscious mind is.

Here's another thing to consider. If you're not in the present moment (and you never are, when your subconscious has taken over), it's darn near impossible to be aware of the voice of your own inner navigation system (a.k.a. your cosmic clues), even when they're screaming at you, trying to get your attention, as Prissy was doing.

The point is this: Your thoughts—and especially the subconscious beliefs that have rooted themselves in you since you were a baby—are powerful. It takes discipline, commitment, and will to replace them with new, more useful ones. It also takes consistent repetition of the new thought, belief, or behavior (especially while you're falling asleep, when your brain waves are most receptive) to make it stick. The more you repeat a new thought or a new behavior, the more it becomes a part of your subconscious. Which, of course, is how you internalized the thoughts, beliefs, and habits that are holding you back in the first place.

You are who you choose to *think* you are. If you think you are insignificant, talentless, and inept, you will manifest those beliefs. So choose thoughts and beliefs that are affirming, positive, and hopeful, that lift you up and help you bring your best self into the world.

You are also who you choose to say you are. The words you speak (and write) are an expression of your thoughts, and of your beliefs, and they are very powerful. If you continue to speak words that limit you, you'll stay limited.

I have a client I'll call Sally who is struggling with assuming the mantle of leadership in her business as a speech pathologist. "Nobody takes me seriously," she says, over and over again. When I suggest she declare herself a leader by introducing herself to others with the words, "I'm Sally, and I run a company called..." she rolls her eyes and shakes her head. "I don't run anything," she says. And so she cements that negative, limiting belief by choosing words that support it.

Another client, who came to me to boost her confidence around presentation skills, repeated the words, "I'm a terrible speaker" several times throughout our first meeting. I knew she'd never develop as a speaker if she stayed invested in that negative belief. And so I immediately insisted she banish that phrase from her vocabulary and replace it with, "I am constantly learning, growing and improving as a speaker." The more she uttered this affirming new phrase, the more she began to believe it. The more she believed it, the more confidence and skill she gained as a speaker.

WRITE YOUR WRONGS INTO RIGHTS

As a life-long journal writer, I highly recommend the act of journaling, choosing to write out your thoughts and feelings on a regular basis. I learned early on that unexpressed feelings tend to fester and grow into obstacles. Writing my wrongs into rights daily allowed me to get a grip on turbulent feelings and to mitigate the sting of frustrating or painful circumstances. This is why one of the first things I ask my coaching clients to do is to buy a journal or notebook dedicated to our work together. I encourage my clients to jot down and complete their homework assignments within the pages of their journals and to use the blank pages as a place to record their accomplishments, thoughts, dreams, and desires with regard to the specific goals they set for themselves. For my clients, the very act of choosing and buying a journal dedicated to their personal growth and development signifies and reinforces a new, more positive way of thinking, believing, and behaving.

Be aware that your words—whether spoken or written—are powerful. So choose to write or speak with words that uplift and empower you. And do it over and over again, until you mean and embrace the truth in your own words.

CHOOSING TO CHOOSE

Again and again, it all comes down to choice. You can choose to take action in the face of your obstacles—whether they come at you from the outside or from the inside (in the form of Moe and Schmoe). Or you can choose to do nothing. Either way you are making a choice. And *not* choosing—like choosing—has consequences.

Mr. Thompson, my high school political science teacher, and possibly the best teacher I ever had, taught me a great lesson in choosing to choose. The country was on the cusp of the 1976 presidential election, a throw-down between Jimmy Carter and incumbent Gerald Ford. Many students in my class, including me, were newly minted eighteen-year-olds facing our first voting opportunity. It was apparent to Mr. Thompson that several of us were apathetic when it came to choosing between the candidates and voting one way or the other. Mr. Thompson patiently helped us understand that by choosing not to vote, we were actually voting. Because our choice to not vote meant one less vote for either candidate—which ultimately affected the voting outcome. In contemporary terms, if you've got a favorite candidate on *American Idol* (ok, I'm a fan, what can I say?) and you choose not to vote for them, and they get voted off, your choice to not vote for them inadvertently contributed to their demise.

In the long run, choosing to choose is more empowering. So choose positive thoughts and beliefs instead of negative, self-limiting ones. Choose to express your feelings—on paper, in words—rather than choke them down or keep them to yourself. Choose to reach out to others instead of isolating yourself and stewing in your own juices. The power to choose is in your hands. Use it wisely.

SAY "AAA"

On a piece of paper, answer the following questions and complete the following suggested exercises:

ATTITUDE

• What is your general attitude about making choices? What do you tend to think or believe about the power to effect change in your life by the choices you make?

• What affirmation can you create, repeat, and embrace to maintain a more positive attitude towards making choices that empower you and move you forward (e.g., "I make conscious choices in every moment." or "I have the power to choose.")?

ACTION

1. If money or any other obstacles were not an issue, what would you choose to do in your life or your work that you aren't currently doing? What choices could you make that would help you make that dream a reality?

2. Write down your top five, self-effacing negative statements or fears, the comments that your little nay-saying gremlins tend to hiss in your ear when you're feeling judged (e.g., "You are too old to be a success!").

3. Now, choose to rework those statements into positive, useful affirmations. Make sure the statements are in the first person ("I") and the present tense, as if they are already a done deal (e.g., "I choose to believe that I am successful, and so I am!"). How does it make you feel to read your affirmations or speak them out loud?

4. Using the positive affirmations you created in exercise #3, write a personal manifesto, or brief mission statement, that expresses your own, strong inner knowing and purpose (e.g., "I was born to use my loving heart, compassionate nature, and gifts as a writer to lift people's hearts and minds. I radiate confidence and clarity in my spoken and written words. I know my truth and am not afraid to speak it. Because I value who I am, others do, too…" etc.). Record it, and listen to it before you fall asleep or prior to an important meeting, conversation, or presentation.

5. What *one* action step are you willing to take this week to embrace and internalize your new, positive affirmations about your ability to choose?

ACCOUNTABILITY
What will you do/what system of accountability will you put into place to help yourself complete this week's step?

CHAPTER SEVEN

Choosing Your Choir

"Gonna find me a choir of everyday angels
Who'll fan my wings so I can fly..."
—ELENI KELAKOS, "CHOIR" FROM *TOUCH THE SKY*

"Find the good ones, and stick with them!"

My college mentor, Jim Barnhill, was referring to people in the entertainment business, when he gave me this piece of advice. Now, after the darkest winter of my young life, as I lurched forward into the light, emotionally spent and broken open, his words had never felt so appropriate. Intuitively, I knew I needed to find what I began to refer to as my tribe, people both in and out of the entertainment industry who genuinely cared about nurturing and supporting the song in me.

Having sung in many choirs, and having enjoyed singing with back-up harmony singers while fronting various bands, I immediately understood the importance of being discriminating and careful about the voices I chose to back up my own. It doesn't take much for a single, dissonant voice to pull a whole choir section off balance. After my run-ins with negative Nellies like Miss Thing, the talent agent, I knew it was more important than ever that I attract and hang around with people who appreciated and supported me for everything I genuinely was.

I had a friend I'll call Janet who, during this time, told me I was wasting my life "shaking your butt, singing in front of drunk people in clubs," and that I was, by and large, too smart to be an actor. I listened to her diatribe for all of a minute. And then I did something unprecedented. I held up a big, fat boundary. "Janet," I said, "I am a professional singer and actress. This is what I love, and what I do. If you don't have anything good to say about it, then we'll have to stop being friends." Janet was actually struck dumb for a good, long and, may I say, highly satisfying moment, and understandably so—I'd never spoken so firmly to her before. When Janet regained her voice, she heartily apologized and promised never to undermine me again. She's been true to her word for over thirty years.

This exercise in boundary setting heartened me. And it was one of the first steps I took in weeding out the nay-sayers from the yea-sayers in my life.

MY PERSONAL CHOIR

Knowing I needed real, unwavering support, I pulled out a sheet of paper and made a list of those I considered real friends—meaning people who would have my back, no matter what. The list was short and included the three close pals I mentioned in the last chapter, Amy, Claude, and Suzi. These were people who I made an effort to spend time with every week or so—people whose mere presence, good humor, and general common sense helped both to ground me and give me wings. These were the people with whom I shared a timeless, energetic connection that my brother and I had, as kids, taken to calling "frequency." You either had—or didn't have—frequency with some-one. And you knew it immediately. When I experienced frequency with some-one, it was as if cosmic electric vibrations of love—and a knowing that felt ancient and strong—were exchanged between us in a figure eight of energy. Frequency occurred instantly, identifying a stranger as an important friend.

I had Frequency with a capital F with Amy, the cornerstone of my trio of choir members. We'd met at a high school theatre competition when, during a lull in the festivities, I followed the sound of Amy's soulful voice to an empty classroom, where she sat perched on a desk, strumming a guitar and belting out a song. We bonded like sisters within a minute of our meeting. Amy and I spent two summers as counselors at summer camp—she, teaching swimming, and me, working as the drama and music lady. We shared tears (mostly over boyfriend issues), great bouts of snorting laughter, and much music together. Amy was (and still is) the best listener I know, and deeply, almost magically, intuitive. When I bared my soul to her about my recent trip to The Edge, she was, as usual, all ears and heart. No stranger to depression herself, she immediately understood what I'd been going through, and simply stood by my side, resolutely there, her kind eyes seeing and loving me for exactly who I was. Even though she lived hundreds of miles away, I felt her continuous presence, through the insightful letters she sent me and the phone calls that always felt like one, long, continued conversation, even when they were interrupted by days or months. Over thirty years later, it's still the case.

Claude, unlike Amy, was a brand new friend—an ex-chorus hoofer-turned-actor, gay, curmudgeonly, grizzled, and lovable. Claude and I met when we were serendipitously paired up for a scene in acting class. I stood at least half a foot taller than him, which we both thought amusing. During the course of our rehearsals, we decided we'd been friends for several lifetimes already and might as well continue the relationship. I spent countless hours drinking black coffee out of French jam jars at Claude's funky apartment in the West Village. After a few, perfunctory *bon mots*, Claude and I would launch into hours-long discussions about purpose, passion, and everything in between. We went deep, fast. Claude, who had retreated from the biz in New York to find himself by doing menial labor and exploring his spiritual side in Santa Fe, New Mexico, had returned to the city with nearly sixty years worth of accumulated wisdom, which he delivered with a dry wit, through clouds of cigarette smoke. I listened. And listened. And listened. And I felt both comforted and stirred alive by Claude's presence.

Suzi, the third in my trio of essential choir members, was, like Claude and Amy, a creative being through and through. Supple and shapely, with skin as pale and translucent as the most expensive marble, her hair shrilly spiked and dyed extreme blonde white, Suzi was a force of nature. She burst into my life at a party of theatre folks, dressed in her signature black—combat boots, ripped fishnets, lacy bustier—big, expressive eyes ringed in kohl. Madonna at her peak had nothing on Suzi at hers (or at any time, for that matter). Delicate, yet fiercely strong, a professional Broadway dancer by temperament and training, Suzi modeled a complete and utter willingness to be exactly who she was. I fell in love with her immediately. At her barely furnished apartment in Brooklyn, she made me German potato salad, shared tales of the Broadway and Off-Broadway shows in which she'd worn the veritable parade of dance shoes—tap, ballet, jazz—lined up against a wall, and held me spellbound with her earthy, sly humor. We met for hours in coffee shops, scribbling timed writing exercises culled from Natalie Goldberg's writing bible, *Writing Down the Bones*. Suzi saw and respected the creative artist in me. And in so doing, she gave me permission to do the same.

This triumvirate of personal choir members did not, you may have noticed, include my immediate family members—my parents, brother, husband. It's not that they didn't love me: I knew they did. It's just that I felt, in my bones, that they didn't quite understand, and might not support, the tremblingly unsteady but determined new me that was unfolding. I couldn't afford any rain on my parade. And so I stayed close to the folks whose voices made mine shimmy and sing with clarity and fervor.

This meant I avoided numerous people whose energy tended to drag me down rather than lift me up: the needy, complaining, compulsive friend who wouldn't ever get off the phone, even after I'd drop gotta go hints like bombs; the artist whose undiagnosed schizophrenia felt like raging, clawing energy whenever she came near; the frustrated whiner, who only ever called to dump her problems onto my shoulders. As politely—but firmly—as I could, I crossed these people off my list of go-to friends. For the first time in my life, I saw the damage I'd been doing to myself as a parts car. And I simply stopped giving my time, my love, or my energy away to just anybody.

EVERYDAY ANGELS

There were other people I allowed into my sphere during this time, other choir members who added their voices to mine from time to time. Often they appeared out of nowhere, with positive, important messages for me to ingest. I learned to pay attention to these everyday angels, and the cosmic clues they often imparted.

Abe, a professional opera singer, would magically appear out of nowhere when I most needed what I can only call spiritual counseling. Interestingly enough, this usually occurred while I was working out—lifting weights at the gym or running laps at a track on the East River. I'd round the bend, and there he'd be, shining his joyous, brown eyes on me like love radars: "Read A *Course in Miracles*," he would advise. "I think there's something in there for you." And so I bought the book and read it; several decades later, I'm still a student of its metaphysical lessons.

"Go hear Eric Butterworth speak at the Unity Church on Sunday mornings at Lincoln Center," Abe would suggest. And so I went. Mr. Butterworth's droll, sensible wisdom filled me with hope and reinforced my growing belief that the power to shape my life was in my hands. The lectures, which attracted enough people to fill the over two thousand seats in the orchestra section of Avery Fisher Hall, always ended with the entire assemblage linking hands, standing up and singing the "Peace Song" ("Let there be peace on earth, and let it begin with me..."). The thrilling energy of our collective voices practically lifted the roof off of the place. I always left Mr. Butterworth's lectures feeling positive and purposeful, and in direct touch with the little voice in me ("Could be more...") that was clearly growing in power and clarity in direct proportion to the attention I was giving it.

Some of the everyday angels in my life, like Abe, flitted in and out of my life with what felt like perfect timing. Others appeared out of nowhere, disappeared without a trace, and changed me forever.

I met one such person while struggling to make ends meet during a forlorn New York winter. I had taken a part time job in the fragrance department at Macy's, standing in high heels for hours on the crowded, marble floor, enticing customers to try a new, floral scent. I was one of a phalanx of smiling, overeager, bottle-wielding perfume spritzers shooting rapid bursts of fragrance at customers, who hurried by, hands raised protectively, heads shaking a vehement "No!" Not liking the feeling that I was assaulting people with spray, I opted instead for quietly brandishing a bottle of perfumed lotion. When a passerby expressed interested in the lotion, I massaged a little onto their hands while we talked (usually about how much they hated being attacked and sprayed by aggressive salespeople). I wound up selling a lot of perfume with this low-key approach.

One afternoon, towards the end of my shift, as my feet began to throb and my mood began to slip into the proverbial toilet, (where, apparently, my acting career seemed to be firmly lodged), I felt a presence in front me. Looking up, I fell right into a steady pair of deep brown eyes. A dark-haired woman of indiscriminate age smiled calmly at me. "I'd love some," she said, nodding at the lotion. I squirted some on her palm and began to knead it into her fingers.

"Why," she asked," are you the only salesperson here who's dispensing lotion instead of perfume?"

"Because I like to touch people," I replied, without thinking.

She smiled even wider. "I knew you'd say that," she replied, giving my hand a squeeze. Then she walked away.

For the ten minutes she was gone, I couldn't get her out of my mind. When she returned, I was, somehow, not surprised.

"I'm going to buy some of that lotion," she said. "Not that I need it. I mostly just wanted an excuse to talk to you again. There's something I need to tell you."

She leaned closer. It felt as if the whole store had suddenly grown silent.

"You're a healer," she said. "Did you know that?"

A healer. I'd never heard that expression before. But intuitively I knew what she meant.

"Yes," I replied, cosmic goosebumps beginning to rise along my spine.

"When you're not working at Macy's, what do you do?" she asked.

"I'm a singer and an actress," I replied.

"What better way to heal," she said. Then she turned and began to walk away.

"Wait," I cried, running after her, "who are you?"

She smiled again.

"Who I am doesn't matter. What matters is what I told you."

Then she was gone, lost in the holiday crowd.

I stood stunned, my body now one big mass of cosmic goosebumps.

"A healer... what better way to heal..."

Talk about cosmic clues.

It would be years before I embraced the fate towards which this everyday angel steered me. But because I had made the decision to open myself up to loving, supportive choir members both permanently in—or temporarily passing through—my life, I had been open to receiving a soul-stirring message that would ultimately transform my life.

MY PROFESSIONAL CHOIR

My list of choir members included not only those from within my personal arena, but from my professional life as well. My agent, Fred, was high on the list. I knew I could trust him to be there for me one hundred percent (he had already proven this to me by suffering through several interminable pieces of experimental theatre as well as countless lunches where I poured out my angst about my slow-building career).

Besides Fred, I was pleased to be able to add a small handful of casting directors, directors, and producers to my list of choir members. These working professionals, several who were of real influence within the business, appreciated the song in me and supported my growth as an actor and performer. Their confidence in me helped me stay resolute and directed.

Carol Reynolds, for example, was one such shining example. A dancer, actor, and teacher, who assisted in the casting of a television commercial for which I auditioned, Carol stayed a gentle, guiding presence in my life for years after our meeting, and I have much to thank her for. Notably, Carol told me I had what she termed "Power, Passion, and Presence," words I posted above my desk as a positive reminder of who I was at my core. Carol also helped me understand there was an essential part of me that I was, unfortunately, still unwilling to reveal. As she described it, it was as if a pane of glass separated the best of me from the rest of the world. I became resolved to break through that pane of glass, and so I began the quest for perhaps the most influential of all my professional choir members—the acting teachers, whose patience, humor, and expertise would lead me, kicking and screaming sometimes, back to my authentic self.

POINTS TO PONDER

In *A Return to Love*, Marianne Williamson's treatise on the book, *A Course in Miracles*, she explains that the purpose of relationships of any kind is to help us grow and learn, heal and be healed. There are three kinds of relationships—

those that last very briefly, like my encounter with the woman at Macy's who told me I was a healer; those that last longer, but not indefinitely (like my relationship with Fred, my agent, which lasted until I eventually moved to California and he, sadly, succumbed to AIDS); and those that last a lifetime (the relationship I share with my brother, George, for example, or my dear friend and foundational choir member, Amy).[6] No matter the length of a relationship—brief or lifelong—or the type that it is—romantic, business related, familial, friend, stranger on the street—or even its nature—adversarial, loving, frustrating, distant, challenging, infuriating—it is there to teach us something. Our relationships are like mini classrooms, rife with learning experiences. The most challenging of relationships—like the toughest life challenges—can often yield the greatest lessons in learning such essential qualities as patience, forgiveness, unconditional love, and non-judgment.

The key to learning while in a relationship—or even realizing that you have met a specific stranger for a specific reason—is remaining as conscious as possible—which is often hard when you're freaking out, yelling, or wanting to retreat with every fiber of your being. Following the feeling down to its roots ("What is this *really* all about? Why did I meet this person? What is there to learn through my involvement or interaction with them?"), and then getting quiet and listening to the little voice in you is essential—if you really want to hear the answer.

Even when I went through that hellish experience with Miss Thing, the hurtful talent agent, I was, thankfully, conscious enough to realize she had something to teach me. For one thing, she taught me that, as a person and as an actor, I had a lot more to learn about how to be fully and authentically present under pressure and scrutiny. She also taught me another valuable lesson: Be discerning about who you consider or designate as a choir member. Better to align yourself with helpers, not hoovers.

HOOVER OR HELPER?

A hoover is someone who sucks the energy, enthusiasm, and passion right out of you. A helper is someone who helps you feel positive and powerful and who celebrates your authentic self.

I had an acquaintance I'll call Dan who was the ultimate hoover. Whenever he deigned to talk to me, he invariably mispronounced my name even though he'd known me for years. He enjoyed teasing me and never looked me in the eye. Worst of all was his habit of whiling away the time by playing a game that involved asking me stomach-turning rhetorical questions like "Which would you rather do: Staple your eyelids shut? Or hammer a nail through your palm?" His gory questions made me very uncomfortable. Still, even as I squirmed and hemmed and hawed, I tried my best to pick an answer. Where-upon Dan would come up with yet another pair of disturbing questions: "What would you rather do: Slam your fingers in a door, or have someone rub your knuckles raw with sandpaper?" The cycle of questions, and the manner in which they were delivered, left me feeling jittery and deflated. And so, one day, as Dan attacked me with another set of strangely violent questions, I simply replied, "Neither," and walked away. That interaction pretty much ended my acquaintance with Dan, for which I was very grateful. Because the following had become very obvious to me: I felt better hanging around positive, loving, hopeful people. So why waste time with people who made me feel the reverse?

I continue this practice of surrounding myself with a carefully selected choir of people whose voices support me—like Mark Le Blanc, my business coach and advisor; my husband, Jim (he is, I'm happy to say, at the top of the list); and, as always, Amy. Does this mean they just yes me to death, or that they aren't honest with me? Does this mean they don't call me on my, well, doo-doo, every once in a while? Heck, no! They hold me accountable for what I say I want to do and for how it stacks up to my deepest values. And they do it in a way that helps me feel deeply valued and loved.

What about you? Are you hanging out with hoovers or helpers? Consider the important people in your life, whether you've known them briefly or for ages. How do you feel when you're around them? Do they suck the happy out of you with their negative, hopeless nature? Or do they pump you up with positive, loving, and hopeful energy? The answer to those questions should help you weed out your choir members so that all that's left are helpers who lend their voice to yours with the most positive, supportive of intentions.

SAY "AAA"

On a separate piece of paper, complete or answer the following exercises and questions:

ATTITUDE

• What is your general attitude about the idea of choosing and maintaining choir members? What do you tend to think, or believe, when it comes to attracting and interacting with your ideal core group of supporters?

• What affirmation can you create, repeat, and embrace to attract and maintain truly supportive choir members (e.g., "Because I value myself I attract valued friends and choir members who value me.")?

ACTION

1. List your current choir members (both personal and professional). Next to their names, write down the value they bring to you, how you feel in their presence, and how or when you tend to reach out to them for support. Who are the top three choir members on this list?

2. Looking at the list, determine which choir members are genuinely helpers and which are actually hoovers. How willing are you to distance yourself from the hoovers on your list and in your life?

3. Who is not on your list of choir members who should be added?

4. If you feel so compelled, write a note to each of your choir members, thanking them for the special way they lend support to your passion, your purpose, and the song in you.

5. What *one* action step are you willing to take this week to encourage yourself to reach out and enjoy the support of your choir members?

ACCOUNTABILITY

What will you do/what system of accountability will you put into place to help yourself complete this week's action step? Which choir member could be a valuable accountability partner for you?

CHAPTER EIGHT

The Gift of Authentic Presence

"If I were me, truly and fully,
Life would be wild and wacky and wooly.
Nothing would stop me,
I'd trust what I feel,
I'd be real, I'd be real, I'd be real."
—ELENI KELAKOS, "IF I WERE ME," FROM *TOUCH THE SKY*

"Well, Eleni. *How do you think that went?"*

Warren Robertson's voice, amped up by the microphone through which he conducts his acting classes, looms large and omniscient. His voice drops down from the darkness in the upper back row of theatre seats. My classmates sit silent, watchful, listening.

I'm shivering in a knee-length, silky slip, barefoot on the dusty floor of Warren Robertson's acting studio, having just performed a scene from O'Neill's play, Desire Under the Elms. Famous actors like Jessica Lange have stood in front of Warren Robertson on this stage, waiting to receive their very first critique for their very first scene. Were they as nervous as I am?

"Tell us, Eleni," Warren's disembodied voice snaking out the darkness makes me jump. "How do you feel about what you did?"

The members of the class—those I can see, anyway—are staring holes in my skull.

"Ok, I guess," I finally reply. My voice seems strangely small.

There is a vast silence, in which I'm left to watch the dust motes float in the milky eyeballs of the stage lights.

Warren speaks again. "Look at you," he says. "You're so striking. You have such presence. We expected so much from you. But instead, you disappointed us."

Disappointed? Disappointed? Did Warren just utter the most hateful, shaming word in the English language, the word Daddy uses like a weapon to put me in my place?

Instantly, my face flames, my eyes lower.

Disappointed? How could this be?

I've starred in plays in high school and in college. And no one ever used the D-word on me. There must be some mistake.

"You were making Saturday morning cartoon faces," Warren continues, "mugging, grimacing, and pushing too hard. Were you aware of that?"

Aware? Of contorting my face like a cartoon character? Heck, no! I'd only been aware of the eyes boring into me from the audience as I performed, and the fact that I felt I was walking through Jell-o, time having slowed to an eerie crawl.

I want to sink though the floor, away from the wall of eyes. I want Warren to stop talking. But he goes on, his voice feeding back through the overhead speakers:

"You didn't so much inhabit the character as you were playing the idea of the character. Which left me wondering, 'Where is Eleni? Who is Eleni? What choices would Eleni make as this character?' That's what we're interested in. We're interested in you. In what you think, in what you know, in what you choose. We don't want to see your idea of this character. We want to see you bring who you are to it."

I am stunned speechless. Nobody has ever told me they want to see me, the real me, either onstage or off. And how the hell do I actually do that?

I stumble off the stage, and out of the glare of the hot stage light, shattered, like a teacup on a marble floor.

So much for my first public performance in a professional acting class.

I know what you're thinking: And you were *paying* that guy to break you into little pieces?

Actually, I was paying him to tell me the truth. As far as breaking into pieces was concerned, well, chaos always comes before change. Birth is always messy. In truth, Warren did me the greatest of favors the day he uttered the D-word: He called it as he saw it. And what he saw was me not choosing to be seen, me not daring to be me.

As painful as it was for me to hear I had disappointed my teacher, it also amazed me to realize he'd been disappointed mostly by my inability and unwilling-ness to bring my true, authentic self to my work. Warren was inviting the real, imperfect me—not some idealized airbrushed fake version—to show up in his class. He made it clear that if I wanted to be a good actress and, frankly, a fully realized human being, I had to learn how to be whoever "me" was— even and especially under the lights, under pressure, and under scrutiny. Talk about a mind-blowing concept.

In the weeks and months I was a member of Warren's class, I worked hard at trying not to work too hard onstage. Warren pointed out that I tended to hold on like a fiend to my idea of a scene or a character, which prevented me from living authentically in the moment. I was, as it turned out, a control freak—a trait that had spawned my bulimic behavior, which was, incidentally, lessening in frequency in proportion to my increased commitment to self-development and self-care. Trying to control everything around me was, it seemed, anti-thetical to being an effective actress. And so, it was necessary that I learn to let go of control—a gargantuan, terrifying, but enthralling task.

One day Warren surprised me by saying, *"I give you permission to have fun, Eleni."* Fun? When was the last time I'd had any fun? And so, for my next scene, from a rather dusty old farce called *Amphytrion 138*, I lightened up considerably. I scuffed around the stage in beat up slippers shaped like raccoons, straightening up my (fictional) home, getting ready for my (fictional) workday, and chatting amiably with my (fictional) husband. Since I wasn't trying hard to do anything except complete that short list of mundane activities, I was shocked by the continuous bursts of laughter from the audience. I wasn't trying to be funny; I was just being me, living in the moment.
Which was the entire point.

When I was done, Warren praised me for bringing my truth to the moment and to the scene. In so doing, he explained, I had created a vivid, memorable character... and I had let my natural sense of humor shine through—without resorting to Saturday morning cartoon faces. "We loved watching you have fun and be you up there," Warren said. "You're a gifted comedienne." I was thrilled, and determined to maintain this forward momentum in my work as an actor and as a person. I resolved to let myself learn to take up my rightful space on the stage and in the world, literally and figuratively. Aflame with these thoughts, I scribbled this poem, this declaration of self.

I see the value
Of a large soul
In a large woman
In a large life
Reaching big, wide, up, out
I can hug the stars
Touch the furthest heart
A big life
Filled fully
Generous
Un-cringing
Of the earth and of the spirit
Huge in its faith
Huge in its love

This is my largeness
My soul
My life
My self

As I began to bring my newfound sense of self to my auditions, I marched two steps forward, one step back. Sometimes I would shine, showing up in all my unique colors, and at other times, I would shut down, my breathing apparatus going awry and affecting my ability to control my singing or speaking. Usually this shrinking or shutting down occurred when I focused on impressing the people auditioning me—especially people I considered powerful and important. I also found myself shrinking and crumpling when I felt underappreciated or undervalued—like when a director got up to answer a ringing phone in the middle of my audition, or a producer noisily unpacked his lunch and began to eat in the middle of my monologue, or a casting director insisted on measuring my height against his to prove I was taller than my resume declared (he was wrong). These unexpected occurrences threw me for a loop and made me retreat into my head, where Moe and Schmoe, my little inner judgers, were waiting to beat me into a pulp ("See? They *hate* you! You're not a *real* actress! Don't you know there are actors a hundred times better than you'll *ever* be! Blah blah blah blah.").

It wasn't until I found a new acting class, lovingly presided over by Michael Howard, my greatest and most influential acting teacher, that I began to get a handle on my inner judgers. Thank God for Michael, the Michael Howard Studios, and the acting class that became my safe and second home.

WHEN THE STUDENT IS READY, THE TEACHER APPEARS

"I'm looking for an acting teacher who won't mess with the essence of who I am!" Those were my very first words to Michael Howard. I was sitting in his office, my long limbs rather defiantly claiming the length and breadth of his ancient couch. He ran his smiling eyes over me and laughed out loud. "Who would want to mess with you?" he asked. He had a point.

When I walked into his class for the very first time, I thought I'd entered a psych ward by mistake. More than twenty-five actors of all ages and body types were lying on the dusty floor, laughing, crying, and making strange sighing sounds. I almost turned tail and ran, but Michael headed me off.

"Lie down on the floor with your colleagues," he said, "and tense and release your body from your toes to the tip of your head. When you release your body, exhale with an AAAAHHHHHHHHHHHH, the kind of sound you make when a doctor examines your tonsils. You'll do this for about fifteen minutes until your body and mind become relaxed, available, and ready to work."

When I looked skeptical, Michael explained, "Look, you're walking around the streets of New York City, trying to be an actress, fighting traffic, hordes of people, and the entertainment business in general. From the moment you get up, from the moment you go to sleep, you're tensing up. The tension is like armor, shutting your body down and cutting off your emotions. In order to do your best work as an actor in this class and beyond, you need to shed that tension and be in a relaxed and emotionally available body. So tense, relax, breathe. Go!"

I did what I was told, feeling like a complete idiot.

After a few minutes, much to my surprise, I found the relaxation exercise freeing, even helpful. I began looking forward to doing it as a prelude to the scene work or exercise work we did before every class. It felt great to cast off the tension that was keeping me so bound up physically and emotionally. The less tension in my body, the more I could breathe. The more I could breathe, the more I could think, which is exactly what I needed to be able to do, if I wanted to bring my best self to my acting work.

It didn't take long for me to put two and two together and apply the breathing and relaxation work to my auditions—particularly during those interminable moments on deck waiting for my name to be called, when my little self-judgers, Moe and Schmoe, were always particularly loud. I'd simply sit—in my audition finery, script on my lap—and slowly tense and release parts of my body—my shoulders, my hands, my jaw, exhaling (quietly, if there were people around) until I was relaxed, but ready. This simple exercise served me by giving me something physical to do: Because fear cannot hit a moving target. Moe and Schmoe, the embodiments of fear, couldn't distract me when I was busy tensing and relaxing my body (which kept me out of my head, where they lived). As a result, I walked into my auditions more centered (physically and emotionally), more in control of my breathing, and better able to focus on what I was there to do—which, as it turns out, was the other piece of the puzzle.

WORKING WITH INTENTION

"Eleni, what are you doing? I don't know what you're doing up there."
Michael's voice is never harsh, just infinitely patient. Sitting at his little table, at the lip of the stage area, Michael waits for my answer. I have none.
"That's the problem, Eleni. Acting is doing. You need to know specifically what you're there to do."

I kick at the dusty floor under my feet, frustrated.

Michael's voice remains calm, "What are you there to do? Make a choice. Keep it simple. Give yourself something specific to do, something you can concentrate on doing."

I think about the scene, from Clifford Odets' The Big Knife, in which I play the unhappy wife of a film actor. I'm there to have a fight with the actor who plays my husband?

No.

I think again. I'm here to tell my husband I'm going to leave him?

Closer. What else?

I try once more. I'm here to tell my husband I'm going to leave him while I clean up the used glasses and dishware from the party we just had?

Michael nods. Bingo!

I try the scene again, focusing simply on clearing up the dishes and tumblers while I deliver the lines I've memorized to my stage husband. Having cleaned up while talking with my real-life husband after parties, I know how to do this. I know this scenario.

Suddenly the scene comes alive. Because the situation is real to me, and my intention is clear (I'm focusing on something specific I can do,) I am fully, authentically present in the moment.
Ladies and gentlemen, Eleni is in the room. Halleluya!

So that's how it's done!

STEPPING INTO THE FIRE, FEELING THE FLAMES

For the next few months, I immersed myself in learning how to work with intention, bringing myself to the moment at hand. When I wasn't performing scenes from plays, I did what Michael called exercise work, culled from his days at the famed Neighborhood Playhouse. One of the most useful exercises was something he called a "Five Object Exercise."

I was to select five simple things to do (e.g., fold laundry, peel a carrot, thread a needle, read two pages in a book, write a grocery list) and then do them silently and thoroughly on stage in front of my classmates. This may sound like the easiest thing in the world to do, but, I assure you, it's painfully difficult with thirty sets of eyes on you. As soon as you realize the audience is watching you sitting there reading that book, self-consciousness sets in like a leg cramp. The flames of fear and anxiety start to lick at your heels. You lose focus, moving away from what you're there to do (reading the book) and begin to focus on your awareness of the audience and on what Moe and Schmoe are hissing in your head ("Your classmates are bored stiff! You're a lousy actor!" etc.). Which is, of course, what happened the first time I attempted the exercise.

Michael, watching like a hawk, leaped in to pull me back on track.

"Ok, Eleni, stop what you're doing." His voice was, as always calm and reasonable. "Breathe. Bring your shoulders up to your ears and release. Breathe. Now look at your audience. Really see them, each person individually. Keep breathing. If you need to, speak out and tell your audience to go away, go away! Tell them to go screw themselves, if that helps. Push them away with your hands! Very good. Breathe again. Now get back to what you are there to do. Simply hold the book in your hands and read the page in front of you. Concentrate on the task of reading. There you go..."

The more I did this exercise work, the more comfortable I became letting people watch me exist in my own skin. I felt safer revealing myself, both publicly and privately.

Following Michael's sage guidance, I began to see each audition and each challenging moment on stage as yet another opportunity to step fully into the flames of fear, feel them crackle around my feet and then–with purpose and intention—walk through the flames to the other side. My reward for making this choice was always the same: A more honest and authentic presence as an actress. This not only gave the people auditioning me a greater and more genuine sense of who I was and what I could do, it gave me the satisfaction of knowing I had allowed myself to feel my fear and shown up anyway. And every time I did, I felt more powerful.

....

POINTS TO PONDER

If there's one thing all my clients have in common, whether they are working with me to reduce fear or anxiety about speaking in public or claiming and sharing their authentic voice in their lives and work, it's the fear of showing up as they really are. Most people believe that if they lead out with their real, foible-filled, human selves, the world will bite them in the butt like a rabid dog. And so they hoist up an alternate self for the world to see; a beta version of themselves that is less authentic, less vital, but, they hope, more accept-able, especially in a work environment. The longer they hold up this false version of themselves, the heavier it becomes. No wonder a client of mine once exclaimed "I'm exhausted from not being myself!"

REVEALING YOUR INNER DORK

It takes courage to show your true colors to others, but the rewards can be great.

I had a client, a successful business owner, who asked me, in all sincerity, if it would be OK for her to reveal more of what she called her inner dork in her interactions with the business community. By inner dork, she meant the part of her that's funny and quirky, blunt and spontaneous—her most delicious, loveable, and memorable essence. She'd recently taken on the presidency of a board of a prestigious business organization and was worried that if she showed her true self, she might not come across as the leader she felt she was. I encouraged her to let her inner dork out to play, and to trust it would help her, rather than hinder her. And so she did, discovering in the process that the more fully she brought herself to her audience and to her business acquaintances, the more comfortable they felt doing the same in return. She led that board, and other boards and organizations that followed, with her inner dork flag flying high, earning a reputation as a leader with edge, spirit, a wicked sense of humor, and the courage to be comfortable with who she is. As a result, her business, that reflects her vital, authentic essence, and attracts clients who want to be around it, is thriving. Best of all, she's discov-ered it's a heck of a lot easier actually being—rather than hiding— who she really is.

We all have an inner dork of some kind—the quirky, unique self we tend to only show our deepest, most beloved friends and family. The more willing we are to trot that side of us out to the greater world, to risk being human and not perfect, the more we encourage others to do the same in return—and that's when real trust, connection, and communication occur.

BEING HUMAN VS. BEING PERFECT

Time and time again I tell my clients, "It's not about being perfect; it's about being human." Time and time again I tell them, "The more you avoid your fear, the more it increases. In order to vanquish fear, you have to embrace it, be with it, and step through it to the other side." Breathing through the fear, helping your body move out of physical lockdown, bringing yourself back to your intention—what you're there to do—is the only process that allows you to richly inhabit the moment instead of running away from it.

I can think of no better way to illustrate this point than by telling you the story of a coaching client I'll call Adam. A jovial and personable businessman, Adam came to me to help him vanquish the fear that ambushed him every time he gave a public presentation. "Eleni," he said, as if confessing a great crime, "I sweat. I mean, I sweat buckets. As soon as I start to realize I am sweating, I sweat even more. And then I am sure the audience is noticing and following every little drop of sweat as it drips down my face, and I sweat even more! It's terrible!"

When he was finished, I suggested a simple plan of action. "First," I said, "go to the store and buy a handkerchief. Not just any old, standard issue white, handkerchief, but one with flair and style. Then fold up the handkerchief, stand in front of a mirror, and practice whipping out the handkerchief, blotting your face, and putting the handkerchief neatly back in your pocket. Do it over and over again until it becomes second nature... and make sure you aren't covering your entire face when you blot it."

Adam eyed me with some uncertainty.

"Then," I finished, "take this handkerchief with you to your next presentation. When you start to sweat, remove it from your pocket and blot your face, as you've practiced."

Adam looked at me like I'd gone crazy. But, to his credit, he did what I suggested.

When he returned for his next visit, he was exultant. "I used the handkerchief as soon as I started to sweat," he said, "and the most remarkable thing happened. I didn't sweat as much!"

I was not surprised. When you shine a light on the five-hundred-pound gorilla in the room, it loses its power over you. Furthermore, Adam's willingness to embrace exactly what was going on (his sweating) allowed his audience to embrace it too—allowing for a shared, rich, and genuinely human experience. This is as true in life as it is behind the speaking podium.

THE VALUE OF AN AUTHENTIC LIFE

It boils down to this. When you're willing to show up, fully and authentically, life actually gets a whole lot easier. You stop struggling against your very nature and step into flow and ease. When you pay attention to what you really need, to whom you really are, and to the cosmic clues that lead you to what you're here to do, you're less inclined to cry out in anguish, like a recent client, "I hate my job! I need a new career!"

When you commit to living an authentic life, in support of your authentic self, you naturally commit to taking the steps necessary to manifest the song in you, so you can sing it to the world!

SAY "AAA"
On a piece of paper, answer or complete the following questions or exercises:

ATTITUDE
- What is your general attitude showing up genuinely and authentically in your life? What do you tend to think, believe, or do when faced with the choice of revealing or hiding your authentic self?

• What affirmation can you create, repeat, and embrace to maintain a more positive attitude towards sharing your authentic self with those around you (e.g., "I am willing to be who I really am.")?

ACTION

1. List your top ten most unique qualities—the things that make you most "you." How comfortable do you feel sharing or showing these parts of yourself to your friends or business colleagues?

2. Recall and write down a circumstance or situation when you were rewarded for expressing what you really felt or who you really are. Now write down how you felt afterwards.

3. How might your life or work change for the better if you were willing to embrace and reveal who you truly are?

4. Find a photo of you as a child in which you appear most alive and authentic. Sitting quietly, use your eyes and your heart to connect with the little you in the photo. Ask little you to help you remember what really matters to him or her: What does he or she love to do? What makes him or her happy? What could you be doing to bring him or her delight and affirmation? Jot down his (or her) wisdom.

5. What *one* action step are you willing to take this week to encourage yourself to show up fully and authentically in your life and work?

ACCOUNTABILITY

What will you do/what system of accountability will you put into place to help yourself complete this week's action step?

CHAPTER NINE

The Gift of Preparation ("Ready...")

"By failing to prepare, you are preparing to fail."
—BENJAMIN FRANKLIN

"Amateurs rehearse until they get it right. Professionals rehearse until they can't get it wrong."
—ANONYMOUS

Question: How do you get to Carnegie Hall?
Answer: Practice, man, practice.

I'd heard that old joke a hundred times; but never did I appreciate the truth in it until I committed to being a professional actress in New York City. The more I auditioned, the more I understood just how important practice and preparation could be to the development and manifestation of the song in me—literally and figuratively. I was, after all, one of thousands of actresses—each one the darling of her high school drama department—living and working in NYC and hoping to be the next great Broadway star. I never before had to worry much about being "competitive, in fighting form" as my agent termed it. But now, I realized, being prepared, being really ready, was the key to a great audition experience—whether or not I got the job. Because the more prepared I felt, the less fear I felt, and the less fear I felt, the more I could surrender to the moment at hand and radiate my most authentic and effective presence—even under the most stressful audition or performance situation.

There was no denying that preparation needed to occur before—not during or after—the curtain rose, the audition began, and my butt was on the line. The more I auditioned, the more I understood and respected this fact. The more I embraced and formalized the rites and rituals that made up my preparation practice, the stronger, more capable I felt.

RITES AND RITUALS, MANTRAS AND MAGIC

Actors, like athletes, dancers, professional speakers, and musicians, are nutty about preparation, sometimes ritualizing it to the point of obsession. In fact, they often feel jittery and uncertain if they skip an element of their preparation ritual. I was—and continue to be—no exception, especially when it came to preparing for an audition.

The cup of coffee in my gloved hand isn't enough to defrost my fingers. I stamp my feet on the frozen sidewalk, and take a quick look at my watch: 6:55 a.m. Five more minutes until the doors open, thank God! I've been standing outside the Actors Equity Building—the professional stage actor's union—on the corner of Broadway and Forty-sixth Street in twenty-five-degree weather since 5:45. There are seven equally frozen actors in front of me and at least sixty lined up behind me. We are here to get a head start on signing up for an open call audition for a musical slated for Broadway. Auditions officially begin at 9:00 a.m. But the earlier we sign up, the less time we'll have to sit around waiting to audition. The less time we have to sit and wait around, the less apt we'll be to psych ourselves out and give a poor audition.

I'm amazed that I actually made it here, considering how much I didn't want to get up when the alarm woke me (and my grumbling husband) at 4:45 this morning. It took every ounce of will to throw off my covers, take a shivering shower, put on my makeup and my audition clothes, gather up my audition material, grab my purse, and slip my way through the light snow to the Eighty-first Street subway station and the CC train, which dropped me off at Times Square in the gray light of dawn.

Someone nudges my behind, and I realize the line is shuffling forward towards doors just swung open. Relieved to move into a warm building, I hurry inside to the registration area where I show my Actor's Equity union card. Signing my name on the audition sheet, I see there are one hundred and fifty slots available today. I am number eight, my lucky number.

Once signed in, I race back out into the cold, conscious of the fact that I need to be back in the building for a two-minute audition I figure will occur around 9:30. I dodge cars and cabs and make my way across the street to the Harlequin Studios, a run-down rehearsal studio that looks like it's been in business since Abraham Lincoln was president. I race up the set of grungy, treacherously steep stairs that lead into the studios and slap five dollars on the counter. In return, I'm assigned a tiny rehearsal room with a rickety upright piano for half an hour, where I practice exercises to warm up my voice for my upcoming singing audition. Up and down the scales I go, working through the early morning cobwebs that are making my voice catch and cough. The more I practice, the more prepared I'll be for my audition. And since every single person auditioning today is going to be giving it his or her best shot, being ready—really ready—is absolutely necessary.

Half an hour later, my voice warm and cobweb free, I race back across the street for my audition. Standing in the short line outside the large rehearsal room where I'll be auditioning, I mentally go over my preparation list: Have I rehearsed my audition song? Yes, every day for the past week, after half an hour of vocal exercises. Do I have my most current 8X10 glossy headshot with my acting resume stapled to the back? Check. Is my audition music within easy access and properly marked? Yep.

I'm now one person away from my audition.
I close my eyes and inhale and exhale three times.
I scan my body for any areas of tension—aha! My neck and shoulders are bunched up in knots. I tense and release those areas, encouraging my body to be relaxed and ready.

I invoke my mantra: "This, or something better!" just as the door opens, and my name is called. Smiling, I walk into the brightly lit audition room, ready to surrender to the stage.

What you just read is not a jumped-up, trumped-up version of what I ideally would have done to prepare for an audition; it's what I actually did, time and time and time again. I did absolutely everything I could possibly do to feel ready—not only thoroughly preparing the material (scripts, monologues, songs), but my body (dance classes, acting classes, regular workouts at the gym) and my mind (meditation, mantras, uplifting self-talk, journaling both before and after auditions, breathing and relaxation work while sitting in the dressing room or waiting room, etc.). Because my voice teacher Patti Allison had informed me that my voice didn't sound as good if I was tired, I even made an effort to get to bed early before an audition (not easy, for a night owl like me). And I did what I could to get to audition venues early so I could familiarize myself with the space and relax into it.

I even took to keeping a little journal to document my auditions. The front of the journal was filled with positive, uplifting statements I could read while waiting to audition. After I was done, I'd immediately record the salient facts of my audition: What I'd worn, who was in attendance, what went well, what had gone wrong, and what I could improve upon. The journal gave me something to focus on and do both before and after my audition. And doing (action) trumps fear (remember, fear cannot hit a moving target).

Once I actually got a job—a play in particular—preparation took on a whole new meaning. Eight hours of rehearsal, six days a week for a month, settling on choices about my character and the script; working with my props (i.e., cigarettes, decorative fans, pens, knives, bullwhips, plates of food, hula hoops) and costumes (bustles, hoop skirts, corsets, harem pants, bathing suits, high heels, tap shoes, jeweled crowns, flowing capes, feathered hats three-feet wide) until I was in control of them rather than the other way around.

Once dress rehearsals and opening night rolled around, a whole other set of rituals kicked in. They included:

Arriving an hour ahead of performance time.

Putting on my makeup (with specific makeup brushes given to me as a gift from cast mates of a previous show), each stroke of makeup helping me assume the character I am playing.

Getting into costume, carefully and meticulously, each piece of clothing helping me feel more in character.

Doing ten minutes of vocal warm-ups.

Doing five minutes of physical warm-ups (or more if I was in a play that required me to dance).

Repeating every single one of my lines out loud really quickly—including song lyrics—just to be sure.

I carefully decorated my dressing area with objects that had meaning to me (a specific checkered table cloth I'd used in all my shows; cards from loved ones; a photo of my husband; gifts from colleagues from previous productions; a rock from a beach where I felt most alive and authentic). These objects helped to ground me and make me feel safer in an otherwise risky and scary situation. So did repeating certain mantras ("I am safe, I am loved. All is well.") and doing breathing and relaxation exercises when I noticed my anxiety level escalating.

And, of course, always exhorting my fellow cast mates to "break a leg" rather than saying "good luck" (I said actors are superstitious) before the curtain went up.

The point is, I did what worked for me, and I swore by it. I made choices that empowered me, that gave me a sense of structure and safety that wasn't necessarily inherent in the given situation. The more I took charge of my preparation, the more confidence I felt, and the better I auditioned. Here's what I wrote in my audition journal (another part of both pre- and post-audition rituals) about my preparation for a callback for the role of a scary, tough prison inmate:

"I prepped well, dressed well for this: cut tee-shirt, midriff showing, no bra, tight jeans, boots, hair in ponytail, ugly harsh makeup. Felt nice to be so thorough. And it paid off. Was off the lines, kept on top of myself, quiet and centered through-out the long wait to be seen this morning, despite the incessant, nervous chatter of another actress in the room. Stayed focused and relaxed, and this at a 9:00 a.m. audition! Despite a forty-five minute wait, I was relaxed and ready due to constant breathing and relaxation work. Didn't chitchat, took my time, felt very present and aware."

Why did I do all of these things? Because I wanted to be ready for whatever happened—no matter what. I was discovering that auditions, like life, always provided a never ending list of unexpected challenges—from audition pianists who butchered my songs, to snarky producers who ignored me while I sang. Regular, ritualized preparation allowed me to utter six, reassuring little words, "I did the best I could." Which was, I realized, enough.

But, in spite of all my careful audition and performance preparation, I was still taking a scattershot approach to my business, following my nose and heart to where they led.
It was time I took more careful aim at what I wanted.
It was time for a plan.

POINTS TO PONDER

As a public speaking coach and trainer, I see it happen time and time again: An otherwise brilliant, capable, established, adult human being stumbling through a sales pitch, formal business presentation, or simple celebratory toast. The cause? Usually a heady cocktail of fear and lack of preparation.

Take the wedding reception I recently attended, where person after person got up to toast the married couple. Relatives and friends rambled their way through heartfelt, though obviously unprepared, speeches. Some fumbled for words; others quickly ran out of steam, unsure about what to say next or how to end.

Then, an eleven year old I'll call Molly, the daughter of the bride, stood up to speak. It was impossible not to pay attention to her. Shoulders back, head high, carrying herself like a queen, she spoke her speech in a clear, strong voice, making sure to enunciate every word. The speech had a clear beginning, middle, and end, and had been thoughtfully and distinctly composed. What was most impressive was how relaxed, centered, and sure of herself Molly was—in direct contrast to the adults who had preceded her.

After Molly was done, I pulled her aside and complimented her on how poised and polished her speech had been. She smiled, shrugged, and said, "I practiced it."

"I practiced it." Three little words that offer a huge insight. Three little words you want to be able to say after every important speech, presentation, and business pitch.

Molly, who belongs to a competitive ice-skating league, learned the value of practicing through the many repetitive rehearsals she skates with her teammates. She's learned that practicing gives her the ability to make a skating routine part of her bones, reducing her fear and giving her the confidence to surrender to her performance. The same holds true, of course, to rehearsing a speech or presentation, and it is holds equally true to developing and mastering the unique song in you—whether it be your skills and gifts as a financial planner, potter, or brain surgeon.

Take it from me (and Molly). Practice changes everything. If you're not taking the time to practice, you're not allowing yourself to improve. You're also robbing yourself from feeling and exhibiting a greater confidence, peace, and poise under pressure.

Practice helps you develop a greater degree of patience. To become a better concert pianist, for example, you have to establish a rehearsal schedule and stick to it over time. Often, lots of time. Carnegie Hall isn't going to come calling overnight. You're going to have to practice umpteen scales and play on several hundred crummy little stages before you're even ready for the bigger stages you're longing to play. But that's ok. Getting as good as you can get right in this very moment is what matters.

Practice leads to mastery. If you intend to use specific talents or skills (like writing, trapeze artistry or number crunching) in service to your purpose (or soul role), it's essential that you hone and develop them. The greater the mastery of your unique skills and talents, the more effectively you can employ them towards actualizing your purpose.

When you commit to practicing, nurturing, and mastering your unique talents and abilities, you embody the spirit behind a phrase attributable to the Ancient Greeks (my ancestors), Aien Aristeuein or *Ever to Excel*. Simply put, this means committing to perform at your highest level in the given circumstance. By allowing yourself to excel—to reach for the best in you so you can touch the sky—you deeply honor the song in you.

The way I look at it, I would never have been able to write this book without all the years of writing practice I had scribbling in journals, penning songs, and composing blogs and articles for publication. Thousands of hours of putting pen to paper (or fingers to the computer keyboard) have helped me find my unique writing voice and given me the confidence to complete the full-length book you're holding in your hands.

What about you? What are you practicing on a daily basis? What are you working to improve so you can be in a position to prevail at your level best when opportunity knocks? Commit to focusing on achieving mastery in your given passion. The more you master your unique gifts, the more relaxed and confident you will be when you're given the chance to share them.

WHAT'S IN YOUR TOOL KIT?

As you can tell from the preparation rituals I performed as an actress, preparation involves more than just getting the material together or achieving the mastery that hours of rehearsal can give you. Preparation also involves getting your head and your heart in the game. Because when you're ready to share the song in you, whether that means pitching your services to a client, picking up the phone to call a potential customer, or delivering a crucial presentation at a conference, you need to be able to do two things: Manage the surge of adrenaline that threatens to broadside you, and smack down Moe and Schmoe, those nasty little naysayers who live in your head and who love to rattle your confidence.

The best way to get your head in the game and feel properly prepared is to ritualize your preparation, just as an actor would. Actors are notoriously obsessive when it comes to preparation rituals. So are athletes—think of Olympic swimmer Michael Phelps and his ritual of listening to music on his ipod before the race, or flapping his arms back and forth across his chest exactly three times before diving into the water. Create a metaphorical preparation toolkit, filled with practices and tools that can calm you down, get you centered, and keep you in the moment.

As an example of a preparation toolkit, let's take a gander at what Rita, a presentation skills coaching client, decided to put in hers.

First of all, rather than simply jotting down the contents of her toolkit on paper, which is what I'd suggested she actually do, Rita took it one step further. She bought a container (a handy little purse) and filled it with physical representations of the tools she chose. Among the items she included were:

• A little picture of a heart given to her by her daughter (a reminder of what really matters—family, love, connection).

• A science award she'd received in school (a tangible symbol of her expertise).

- A silicone wristband embossed with the word "Breathe." (The wristband, which she'd received along with my Let Go of the Armor breathing and relaxation audio exercise, was a reminder for her to use her breath to get centered and relaxed).

- A laminated nametag (to remind her of her ability to reach out and connect deeply with others).

- A little container of water (so she'd remember to stay hydrated because her mouth gets dry when she's under pressure).

These are things Rita can touch, look at, or do to help her stay focused, breathing, relaxed, and in the moment—items that help her *touch the sky* in a pressurized situation. It's important the items in her toolkit have meaning and significance to her. And it's equally important she use them, regularly and ritualistically, whenever she approaches an environment or circumstance where she might be tempted to play small.

SIP YOUR DIVA JUICE

Here's another client-inspired example of something you might want to throw into your personal preparation toolkit: diva juice.

I recently facilitated a day-long presentation skills workshop, which culminated in each participant delivering a five-minute speech. One of the participants, an animated young woman named Dinah, gave an inspirational speech about the power of perseverance. Dinah talked about wanting to be a runner, like her dad, and the years it took to get to the point that she could run marathons without quitting. She did anything she could to encourage herself to hang in there with her running, including listening to hip hop music with lots of swear words prior to hitting the track—get-up-and-go-music that, she explained, made her feel like a "bad ass." Dinah's dad supported her efforts by having her apply what he called anti friction gel and energizing gel to help make the act of running more pleasant and appealing to her.

Whether the gel actually worked or not, the idea of it was enough to give Dinah the added boost she needed to commit to her running. It struck me that Dinah could apply this same concept to the anxiety she was experiencing as a public speaker, and so I suggested she go out and purchase some great smelling gel or lotion, and rename it "bad ass gel." I told her she should apply the gel prior to a speaking engagement as one of a series of ritual preparation activities (like listening to her beloved hip hop music) as a way of helping her feel like a bad ass speaker, capable of tearing up the speaking platform.

The idea was met with great enthusiasm, and it prompted, Melinda, another bright young woman, to throw in her own variation. "I know," she declared, holding up the bottle of water I had insisted was a necessary part of every presenter's toolkit (hydration, hydration, hydration), "I'm going to rename my bottle of water 'diva juice!' So every time I take a sip of water before or during my presentation, I'll be upping my diva quotient!"

When the laughter subsided, one thing was clear: Do and use whatever works to help yourself feel ready. That not only goes for prepping for a stressful speaking engagement, but for preparing yourself to handle the challenges in your everyday life.

Nothing boosts your level of confidence like being ready.
Nothing shuts down your little naysayers more effectively than being ready.
And nothing serves your passion and purpose more than being ready.
Because only when you're ready—really ready—can you take full advantage of the opportunities that come your way.

So take the time to prepare thoroughly, ritualistically, and well. You—and the song in you—are well worth the effort.

SAY "AAA"

On a piece of paper, answer the following questions or complete the following exercises:

ATTITUDE

• What is your general attitude about preparation? What do you tend to think, believe, or do about the act of preparing?

• What affirmation can you create, repeat, and embrace to maintain a more useful attitude towards preparation (e.g., "Because I am ready, I feel confident.")?

ACTION

1. Are you a preparer or a procrastinator? In general, how prepared do you need to be to feel confident about a task or a presentation you are about to perform?

2. What's in your preparation toolkit? What do you need to do, to have, or to implement to feel most physically and mentally prepared to perform at your best?

3. What do you know you need to prepare or practice further or with more consistency to move yourself to authentic excellence in your chosen area of passion, expression, or expertise?

4. What *one* action step are you willing to take this week to help yourself prepare for a task/a presentation/a goal or to develop a skill with more consistency and commitment?

ACCOUNTABILITY

What will you do/what system of accountability will you put into place to help yourself complete this week's action step?

CHAPTER TEN

The Gift of Planning ("Aim...")

"Dreaming, after all, is a form of planning."[7]
—GLORIA STEINEM

"Sang for the world
Was Happy
Gave"

I stare at this collection *of words, hastily scribbled on a sheet of yellow lined paper, written in response to my friend Gary's question, "What three things would you like people to say about you when you're dead and gone?"*

A show biz veteran, Gary has promised to help me hone my focus so I can take a more consistent approach towards getting work as an actor. The goal setting tool I am currently exploring is something he swears by.

I have never done this before, plucking my dreams from my mind and pinning them concretely onto a piece of paper. This, it seems, is planning. I mean real planning, the kind that people who actually want to get things done actually do.

I like it.

"Now," Gary instructs, "imagine your ideal day, when everything you're working for comes to fruition. Write down all the details, as if you're living it right now."

I joyously scribble down a paragraph describing a magical day that includes my playing the lead in a fabulous new musical at the Kennedy Center in Washington, D.C., my favorite professional theatre, followed by a celebratory party with great food, drinks, and my closest friends and family members. By the time I put my pen down, I am filled with energy, hope, and excitement for what lies ahead.

"Now," says Gary, "write down three to five things you want to have accomplished in ten years that will move you toward that ideal day. Don't think about it, just write. Go!"

My hand automatically jots down a few goals. This is fun!

"Now, write down three to five things you want to have accomplished five years from now."

I eagerly follow Gary's lead.

He asks me to do the same for two years, then one year, then six months. Then, more concretely, for one month. One month? I can practically see the month stretched out ahead of me.

"Ok," he says, "now write down one to three things you intend to accomplish in one week." I do.

"In one day."

I look up. One to three things I can do today? That's, well, immediate.

"When you write things down," Gary explains, "they tend to have more weight. So, write down what you want to accomplish."

As a writer and a list maker, this makes total sense to me. My hand sails across the paper.

Gary smiles and peers at my scribbles.

"There's a nice balance between the personal and the professional," he nods approvingly. "These words represent the goals you're reaching for and the steps you need to take each day in order to create the life and the work you want. The key is to take steps every single day, no matter how you're feeling.

"Look at it this way," Gary continues. "If you owned a donut shop, and you didn't feel like getting up to make the donuts, there wouldn't be any donuts to sell, and you'd be out of business in no time. You are the owner and chief cook and bottle washer of the donut shop called You, Inc. So, get up and make the donuts."

He hands me back my list of goals.

"Those goals," he says, poking at the paper, "are your targets. Now let's help you take better aim at them."

He slaps a little paperback booklet into the palm of my hand. I recognize it immediately: It's a copy of the Ross Reports, the trade publication that lists New York City's legitimate talent agents and casting directors. My own copy of the Ross Reports, which I've been referring to for months, is filled with question marks. While the publication has helped familiarize me with the names and locations of talent agents and casting directors operating in Manhattan, it's mostly served to overwhelm me. Every time I leaf through it, I am not only stumped by the sheer number of possible contacts, but how to most effectively approach them. Which of them, I wonder, is the best fit for me? After all, I've only met a few of the people listed, either by chance or at auditions. The rest are simply faceless names on paper.

"How many people do you know personally in this book?" Gary asks, as if reading my thoughts.

Sheepish, I name half a dozen.

"Not enough," Gary says. "Let's change that."

For almost an hour, I scribble madly while Gary flips methodically through the book and points to people he knows well enough to recommend. I put a star next to the names of the people he is adamant I meet. "Use my name when you contact them," he insists. Just as adamantly, he steers me away from those whose reputations aren't stellar or who might be a poor fit.

When we're done, he gives me a big grin.

"First, you've got to know where you're going," he says, gesturing both to my list of goals and to the little book I'm clutching to my heart. "You can't take aim unless you have a target, right?"

I may be young, but I recognize the incredible gift Gary has freely given me. Not only has he helped me understand the value of treating the acting biz like a business, but he's hammered home the value of setting goals. And by aiming me at the right people, he's helping me waste less time in the pursuit of those goals. I can't help but hug him.

"Ok," he says, squirming out of my grasp, "the rest is up to you. Get up and make the donuts. Take aim and take action. Make the people you've starred in this book your new best friends. Give it everything you've got."

And so I did. Prepared by acting classes, voice lessons, and dance classes and armed with a solid plan and a target to aim at, I swore to treat myself and my work like a donut shop with an actual storefront. I challenged myself to get up every day and make the donuts, whether I felt like it or not. I vowed to take daily, consistent steps to make my passion and my purpose a reality. Because all the passion, purpose, preparation, and planning in the world cannot replace taking action when the time is right. After all, we don't say ready, aim, *pause.*

We say ready, aim, *fire.*

POINTS TO PONDER

Imagine a football game without goal posts. The ball would be passed to no particular player for no particular purpose. Both players and fans would eventually get discouraged, frustrated, and bored silly, and the game, such as it is, would be abandoned.

Goal posts give the players (and the fans) something towards which they can focus their efforts and attention. Without those goal posts, the game would be a meandering dud.

In football, as in life, if you want to get the ball from *here* to *there*, you have to determine what *there* is. You have to make *there* as clear and compelling as you possibility can.

Then you have to map out the steps that will take you *there*; and, finally, you have to keep going forward with the ball, no matter how many big ol' nasty, smelly linebackers try to pound you into the ground.

This is why, during my first career planning session with Gary in New York so many years ago, he started me out by first asking me to metaphorically create my goal posts. The vision or picture I created with my words—"Sang for the world. Loved. Gave." or "Playing the lead in a musical at the Kennedy Center, celebrating with my beloved friends and family"—got my passion soaring. In that energized, enthusiastic state, laying out a focused plan to achieve my vision was an easy and welcome next step.

PASSION FUELS YOUR PLAN

Your passion must be ignited before your plan is either put in place or executed. As discussed in chapter nine, knowing your intention (the aim or purpose that guides your action (*why* you are doing something) keeps you focused and on task. And when your intention hitches itself up to your passion it becomes an unparalleled driving force, egging you on towards your goals.

Which is why, when I'm working with coaching clients, my intention is to activate their passion by helping them create a clear, focused and compelling vision they can work towards. That's where the act of planning begins. Because, as noted feminist and activist Gloria Steinem said, "Without leaps of imagination or dreaming, we lose the excitement of possibilities. Dreaming, after all, is a form of planning."[8]

VISION VA-VAVOOM

During out first session, whether I'm helping someone become a more confident speaker or create a more fulfilling career, my initial question is always the same: Why are you here? What do you want to get out of our time together?

Once we've nailed down the intention (the *why*), it's my job to coax a compelling vision (the *what*) out of my client—the more detailed the vision, the better.

If I'm working with a presentation coaching client, I lead him through a series of questions designed to help him weave a detailed vision of the confident, persuasive speaker he has the potential to be. Once my client articulates this compelling vision, he invariably becomes even more psyched about achieving it.

When I'm working with a life or career coaching client, I take this visioning process a step further. I ask my client to close her eyes and imagine waking up five years from now on the morning of her ideal day. I instruct her to take me through her day as it unfolds around her, describing out loud what she sees, feels, hears, tastes, and smells. I direct her to speak in the present tense, as if what she wants to create is already a done deal. I capture on paper what she shares with me, type it out, and read it back to her at our next session.

My clients are often floored and moved by the specificity and the clarity of details offered up by their own subconscious mind. And they get excited— really excited—about what they can potentially create. Which helps them move ahead, through the tougher task of determining—and then taking—the steps towards the vision they've articulated.

If you're not working with a coach, you can ask a trusted choir member to listen and take notes while you speak your vision out loud. Or you can turn on a recording device, sit quietly, close your eyes, and process through the exercise out loud, transcribing your vision to paper when you're through.

Another particularly fun and creative way to nail down your vision is to put together a vision board. This involves taking a large piece of poster board and covering it with images and words that evoke what you are trying to create. You can focus on one area of your life (i.e., your career or your speaking abilities) or more than one (i.e., relationships, health, spirituality). Choosing images that evoke a feeling in you is most essential. The mere act of under-going this process, of attracting to you and pulling together the elements that evoke your dream, sets the completion of the dream in motion. And, when you place it somewhere you'll see it often, your vision board acts as a very palpable daily reminder of what you are in the process of creating. If this appeals to you, there are many excellent books available giving you an idea of what a vision board might look like and how to get started. There are even online tools available to help you create a vision board on cyber paper.

The point is this: Creating a compelling vision can kick your passion into high gear, putting you into a far better position to lay out an effective plan and make it a reality.

PUTTING THE PLAN IN PLACE

Once I've worked with a client to establish their vision, I do with them what Gary did for me so many years ago when he taught me the essentials of treat-ing Me, Inc., like a donut shop: I help them determine the steps they need to take to actually achieve their desired outcomes.

There are several ways to approach visioning out your passion and purpose and then mapping out the steps you need to take to make them a reality.

ly friend Gary's system involves initially describing your vision (or goals) in detailed, written form. Then, working backwards from the compelling vision, you lay out the sub goals and steps to take to reach those goals in ten years, five years, two years, one year, six months, one month, and one week from now. End with a brief list of action steps you can do today. I used Gary's process for years and found it incredibly useful.

But since working with Mark LeBlanc, my business coach (www. smallbusinesssuccess.com—I admit, I adore him, and this is a shameless act of promotion), I have been incorporating his planning and execution methodology to even greater effect. He has made me—a diehard fan of multiples of two and four—fall in love with multiples of three (thirty-, sixty-, and ninety-day increments, and three daily high value activities). More specifically, Mark has taught me to work in successive thirty-day cycles instead of thinking in yearly chunks. As Mark puts it, "It's a New Year every thirty days!"

At the beginning of each thirty-day cycle, I make choices about what steps I want to complete in support of my ultimate goal (Mark calls those steps "benchmarks). And then, every morning, I break the process down further by making a list of three marketing steps to complete in support of my benchmarks. I ask myself, "What three things will I do today to touch the sky and reach my goal of _____?" Then I complete those steps, with as much commitment as I can muster, no matter what obstacles pop up (and, as already discussed, there is always an obstacle panting in the wings, waiting to pounce).

As someone who used to pen endless to-do lists I could never finish, facing down a short list of three things—e.g., a follow-up sales phone call, two hours of writing my blog, attending a networking event—is something I can handle. I can handle doing three things. Heck, if I somehow can't do all three things, I can at least do one thing from the list. After all, the pyramids were built one brick at a time. What's important is that I determine and take clear, strong action steps in support of a goal, setting me up for a greater chance of success.

I use this same approach with, in particular, my Blue Sky Coaching clients, handing them cheery little task pads pre-printed with these words

"What will I do today to TOUCH THE SKY?"

1.   Yes___ No___

2.   Yes___ No___

3.   Yes___ No___

I instruct them to jot down three things in support of the goal they're working towards. Then, I suggest they ask themselves at the end of the day if they have, indeed, completed those tasks, checking off Yes or No in the spaces provided.

Completed all three tasks? Good for you. Only one? That's fine. None? It is what it is—don't beat yourself up about it. Just crumple up the paper and toss it out. Start afresh the next morning.

It's simple. But it works.

GETTING READY TO GET READY

Once I've determined what my clients want to create or achieve, and established the steps that will help make their vision a reality, they're poised to take action. That's when we move into what the next chapter is all about: Taking action—letting the arrow fly towards specific targets. My clients are, after all, essentially paying me to hold them accountable for actually *doing* what they say they want to do.

Here's where it gets tricky: Planning (which is a component of preparation) is an essential part of any successful enterprise (or presentation, for that matter). But it can also stop people in their tracks. It's truly remarkable how many people get stuck in the process of planning and never actually take action. I call that "Getting Ready to Get Ready." It's an affliction experienced by far too many people, closely akin to the perils of limbo.

Imagine this scenario: You decide to commit to a regular workout that involves a nice mixture of running, weights, and yoga. Wanting to lay down a plan you can adhere to, you spend two hours laying it all out in calendar form on a gigantic piece of paper... ten sit ups there... two miles of running there... one hour of yoga there. Dissatisfied with the look of the finished workout chart, you make a new one, using a ruler to make the calendar lines straighter. Then you spend another hour decorating it with cute little drawings and stickers. Satisfied, you post the paper on the fridge. Until you have the urge to rework it and get it just right yet again. You work it and work it and work it, neglecting to do what the plan is geared to get you to do: Work out. Sound familiar?

I have a client – a very talented budding speaker who came to me for help in putting together his signature keynote presentation so he could launch a professional speaking career. In the eight months we've been working together, we have spent hours and hours setting, then scrapping or revising, his initial keynote idea. That's because every time we get near to its completion, my client comes bursting through the door with a new approach he wants to try, or a different theme he wants to weave through the material. He's never quite ready to end the process of planning and preparing and begin taking action to market and present his keynote speech. As a result, I have recently had to dig my heels in as a coach, pointing out to my client that he is holding himself back by remaining in a constant state of preparation. It's time to stop dancing around the next step, which is to book some speaking gigs so he can air out his material and move forward. He has planned enough: Now it's time to execute.

Don't get stuck getting ready to get ready. Planning is essential. But it doesn't take the place of execution and persistent action. You can't just plan the work. You've got to work the plan.

SAY "AAA"

On a piece of paper, answer the following questions and complete the suggested exercises:

ATTITUDE

• What is your general attitude about planning? What do you tend to think, believe, or do when faced with having or needing to plan?

• What affirmation can you create, repeat, and embrace to maintain a more positive attitude towards the act of planning (e.g., "Because I take the time to plan, I know where I'm going.")?

ACTION

1. What types of tools or techniques do you use to help you determine or create a plan?

2. What tends to keep you from honoring a plan you have in place?

3. Recall a time in your life when you effectively put a plan in place. How did it help you achieve your goals? How could implementing a specific plan change your life or affect your work for the better?

4. Using the visioning suggestions in the Points to Ponder section of this chapter, create a compelling vision in words or images for what you want to create in your career or life.

5. Using one of the two planning suggestions in the Points to Ponder section of this chapter, create a simple, written plan to move you ahead towards your vision.

6. What *one* action step are you willing to take this week to create and honor your plan?

ACCOUNTABILITY

What will you do/what system of accountability will you put into place to help yourself complete this week's action step?

CHAPTER ELEVEN

The Gift of Persistent Action ("Fire...")

"If you wait too long for the perfect moment, the perfect moment will pass you by"
—FORTUNE COOKIE

ON ONE HAND...

I followed Gary's advice to be a donut shop, leaping out at the world, guns blazing, plan in hand. Amazingly enough, Gary's organized, simple approach to moving my business forward worked for me. I included marketing approaches to a specific target such as postcard campaigns to theatrical and casting directors letting them know of upcoming performances or just saying "hi," and bi-weekly visits to casting agencies and agents, dropping off my photo and resume and simply saying, "hello." I worked out and vocalized daily, and took acting classes and voice lessons on a regular basis. Regular, consistent action seemed to be the key.

The daily, weekly, and monthly goals and steps gave my life a much-needed structure. And, oddly enough, the structure made me feel both safe and free.

When I thought about it, I realized it's like the cordoned off, designated swimming area at the beach. Staying within the ropes, while initially seeming restrictive, ultimately gives both the swimmers and lifeguards a greater sense of freedom. Swimmers can swim and splash with joy and abandon within the given area, and lifeguards, in turn, are freed from the stress and worry of monitoring unmanageably vast quantities of ocean.

Years later, the brilliant theatre director Anne Bogart would summarize that notion to me in five little words: "There is freedom in the form." There was, indeed, freedom in the structure I created for treating my career like the business it was, with a prescribed and defined order of chosen daily activities all designed to advance myself as an actress.

My friend Gary was right. The more I took consistent action, towards a specific outcome, the more I moved forward. The less I took consistent action, the less specific the outcome, the less I moved forward.

This was, I realized, almost identical to the process I'd learned to embody in acting class. Set your intention. Make bold, specific choices in support of that intention. Then go for it, full tilt boogie.

And, as always, the choice was up to me.

I had to hold myself accountable for the actions I chose to take.

Even—and especially—on the days when no's came thick as horseflies at a picnic.

Which, as it turn out, was most days.

ON THE OTHER HAND

"You didn't get the part. They went in another direction."

"It was between you and one other woman. They really loved you, though!"

"They went with a short blonde woman… the director's niece, I think…"

"The director said you weren't pretty/young/short enough..."

"Your boobs weren't big enough."

"They scratched the whole project... but the director swears he'll keep you in mind for other projects..."

These were the kinds of phrases I heard almost daily from Fred and the other agents who represented me. They all boiled down to one word—no. In spite of how often I heard that word, it had the power to wound me with fresh fangs each and every time I heard it.

H.B.O? HELL NO!

"You got the part!"

Are there sweeter words for an actor to hear? Nope, I don't think so.

"You got the HBO movie! You're going to Israel to shoot Steal the Sky!*" My agent's voice is jubilant.*

I scream with happiness, dance the phone around the room. This is a big deal. This is my big break.

"Make sure your passport's valid," he continues, "you'll be leaving in two weeks."

I got the part! After two months of auditioning, I got the part—the vivacious, French wife of a diplomat, pal to Mariel Hemingway's character, in this HBO thriller! And, it seems, I beat out some pretty heavy-duty actresses, including one who is actually French!

I got the part! And best of all, I get to go to Israel to shoot it—a country that shaped me and that I haven't seen since I was fifteen. I can't believe my good fortune.

I don't think I've ever been happier.

For the better part of a week, I prance about on a sparkling cloud of happyhappyjoyjoy, telling everyone I know—my parents, my brother, my friends, the mailman, the cashier at Gristedes Market—the good news: I got the part! I got the part! I got the part!

Then, the phone rings.

"They need to see tape," my agent says.

What? Huh?

"The suits at HBO need to see some tape on you. You know, just some clips from other parts you've done on screen. Just to be sure."

Sure? How much more sure could they be? They cast me, for Pete's sake!

Spooked, I knock myself out calling directors I've worked for, begging for a little piece of tape here, a little piece of tape there, evidence of my as-yet limited work in TV or film. I knock myself out further paying a video editor to put it all together for me.

The tape flies off to the suits at HBO in California.

Now comes the wait.

Three days go by. Not a word from the producers.

A week passes, seven agonizing days. Still no word.

My agent starts sounding both annoyed and worried when he takes my calls.

"Nada, not a peep," he says "but I know they asked Abe Vigoda from that TV show Fish for tape too."

This is supposed to comfort me?

On a particularly grim winter day, wrung of color and hope, my agent finally calls. He is matter-of-fact.

"You're not doing it."

My heart rips open, just like that.

"They're picking an Israeli actress. It'll save them some money."

There's a pause. I can hear my agent shuffling through papers. "Hey," he says, "they turned Abe Vigoda down too!"

But I am not listening. My head feels hot and empty except for a mocking phrase from a Stephen Sondheim song from A Little Night Music: *"Every Day a little death..." That's how it feels to not get a role for which I've auditioned four times, that was formally offered to me, and that has now, unceremoniously been taken away: Like a little part of me is dead.*

Blah blah blah. My agent is still talking. I clunk the phone onto the receiver, crumple to the floor, and cry like a small child.

No.

Again.

SAME OLD, SAME OLD

NO. No. No. No. No. No. No.

Sometimes the no's came so fast and hard it was like being caught in a flurry of jabs and uppercuts. At other times, they sidled up to me with a seductive smile, pulled me close, and then punched me hard in the gut. Always, they undid and overwhelmed me.

A big no, like the HBO debacle, could hold me hostage like a terrorist with a gun to my head. And, in spite of well-meaning people trying to help me feel better by saying things like, "You can't take it personally," or "It's just an audition," the pain of the loss sat in my bones like a virus. I had to work it out of my system for a few hours, a day, two days, whatever it took.

In spite of loads and loads of passion and purpose, preparation and what appeared to be a great plan on paper, there were days like the day of the HBO debacle, when the sheer number and the severity of the no's just made me want to pull my covers over my head. And so I did.

BACK TO THE BASEMENT

Clobbered by rejection, I moped and pouted and hid and earnestly examined the question "Should I stop trying to be a performing artist? Am I barking up the wrong tree?"

But after the requisite number of hours or days spent snuggling up with what I've come to call my blanket of doom, I eventually got back to working the plan, back to taking concrete, consistent action. Because there was one thing I was learning: I couldn't get an acting job without auditioning. And the longer I sat at home feeling sorry for myself, the fewer auditions I was going to get.

The good news was this. The more willing I was to take consistent action the less I was ambushed by fear, uncertainty, and doubt. Because, as I've said twice before (it bears repeating), fear really can't hit a moving target.

POINTS TO PONDER

You know what it's like when you begin to build your dream—whether it's to improve yourself as a speaker, learn and grow a skill, or create your own business. You start out all excited, arranging the little nook in the back of your house to your liking—a new desk from IKEA, a refurbished laptop, a perfect full-spectrum light lamp. You get that logo made, those business cards printed up. Bursting with passion, you tell everyone you know about your new undertaking. Your spouse, kids, and friends are in full support, on board with your new schedule and your new activities.

It all goes swimmingly. Until it doesn't. You blow through your list of contacts and run out of leads; you make ten phone calls to warm leads and nobody calls you back; you practice your new pitch or presentation at a small networking event, and not one person comes up afterwards to talk to you. And then summer hits, and the kids are home for three solid months, and they look to you—because you are working out of the nook in the back of the house—to schlep them from one activity to the other. And, of course, you do. At which point, the newly tacked together foundation of your new business begins to crumble.

The no's can feel downright overwhelming. And if you don't have a system in place for handling them, for helping yourself persevere in spite of resistance or obstacles, you'll stagnate, stop, and stay stuck.

That's why it's so important to take regular, daily steps forward even (and especially) when you don't feel like it. Consistent action is the key to moving with persistence through obstacles and resistance.

My friend and client Betsy Volaric learned the value of doing just that.

GET BACK TO THE BASICS: BETSY'S STORY

When her husband left her out of the blue, with two infants to raise and very little financial support, Betsy instantly turned from stay-at-home mom to car salesperson. It was 1984, and Betsy was one of the first women selling cars on her lot (or on any lot, for that matter). Within six months, she had broken the corporate record for gross profit in monthly sales.

"For a while, I was on top of the world," Betsy recounts. "I was selling lots of cars, paying my bills, and was even recognized at the Christmas party. Soon after, the owner took me aside and said, 'You did really well last month. But remember, that was last month. In the car business, each month you start back at zero. Let's see how you do this month.'"

Betsy's personal Moe and Schmoe nay-saying gremlins loved that remark. Seeds of self-doubt were firmly planted, kicking off the beginning of the slippery slope that led to her first big valley in the peaks and valleys of sales.

Betsy continues, "I started to struggle. The guy next to me was selling cars like crazy, but I couldn't put a deal together to save my life.

"I started to worry... 'I have a family to support, bills to pay, I'm on 100 percent commission... What if I don't sell anything? I won't be able to pay my bills!'

"Worry turned to fear... Maybe it was all a fluke? Maybe they were right, and I couldn't really sell; I had just been lucky!

"Fear turned to panic. I turned to my friend, a woman and mentor who had trained me.

"She said 'Of course you can sell! You've already proven that! You just need to get back to the basics.'"

Betsy went home and thought about her friend's words. She decided that for the next few days, she wasn't going to even *think* about selling a car. With each customer, she was going to pick a part of the sales process and do that one part the very best way she could.

"After I was done with my customers," she says, "I would critique myself and figure out how to do it better the next time. When I mastered that step, I went on to the next one. I didn't measure my success on whether I sold a car but on how well I mastered that part of the sales process. Sure enough, after a few days I started selling again, and I was back on track."

Betsy discovered that by shifting her focus from the fear of failure to some-thing she could control, moment by moment, she boosted her confidence and helped herself get back in the game. Once she focused on simply connecting with the customer and listening well, her sales skyrocketed.

JUST DO ONE THING

As Betsy demonstrated, when you're feeling squished under the heel of life, dialing down to the basics and doing a few simple things—or even one simple thing—within your control can help you slowly crawl out of the basement and back into action in the greater world.

My spiritual counselor and life coach, Sanda Jasper, helped me understand the value of dialing down and doing one simple thing. When I called her on a day I was feeling so blue I could barely get out of bed, she suggested three simple actions:

1. Move from where you are to somewhere else—if you're in bed, for example, get out of bed. If you're in one room, move into another room; if you're inside, move outside.

2. Reach out. Call someone, talk to someone, share your feelings and concerns with someone else (as I had done by calling her).

3. Journal it out—write out your feelings (as I suggested in chapter six).

Back when I was struggling with being rejected for the HBO movie, I con-tinued to do the basics every day, even if I didn't feel like it. I did my vocal exercises, I went to the gym and worked out, and I wrote in my journal. Each time I took action on my own behalf, I felt a little better. The key is to keep it simple, and to just do it—no matter how you're feeling or how much you-know-what is flying around you.

STOKING THE FIRE

Helping yourself persevere through challenges, change, and obstacles means taking consistent action—and not just action that moves your dream forward, but action (and activity) that soothes, nurtures, and centers you. The world is filled with activities and opportunities that can keep the flame of your passion and purpose stoked and burning. These activities can be solitary, like meditating, reading an enlightening book, or taking a long walk on a beautiful beach. Or they can be social activities, like sharing a meal with a cherished choir member, taking a yoga class, or playing a silly board game with your favorite niece. The possibilities are endless. What's most important is that the activity you choose to do elevates your energy, mind, and spirit and fans the flame of your passion and purpose, honoring and affirming the song in you.

As I was writing this chapter, I had the notion to reach out to my friends and clients and ask them what actions they take to help themselves persevere in the face of no's. The responses were as varied, wise, and wonderful as the people who shared them. Here are a few nuggets:

Miche Suboski, visionary coach, consultant, and president of Kai Business Solutions said, "I settle myself into a safe place and imagine my twenty years older self. I know she is wiser, more patient and at peace with herself. It helps me to become her in the moment."

Suzi Winson, the foundational choir member I mentioned in chapter seven, now a trapeze artist, clown, and partner at Circus Warehouse, a school that teaches those arts wrote, fittingly, "Practice something."

Kevin Gillespie, coach, speaker and radio host, said "I have a little parlor trick for perseverance that I invented as a kid for going to the dentist. I used to tell myself that whatever hurt in the dentist's office would only hurt while I was in his chair. Second by second and minute by minute, I knew it would be over soon. Today, with anything that I find difficult or even painful, I focus on the fact that as soon as I'm done with it, it's over."

Emily Hay, founder of Hay There Social Media, wrote, "I have always liked the phrase 'Hold the rope.' To me, it symbolizes that when all else gets complicated and it becomes hard to see your goal through the complex challenges, that as long as you 'hold the rope,' you won't fall off or get lost on your way to your goal. Stay true to your plan, hold the rope. Even if you don't have the mental energy to charge forward, simply hold the rope and you will stay on track, things will be ok."

Delfina Bonilla-Cassel, personal trainer, yoga instructor, and owner of En-Forma Fit, declared, "I blast a favorite album and sing at the top of my lungs."

Sandra Carter, psychologist and life/career coach wrote, "I go back to basics, and re-connect with why I'm here and what I'm called to do—this inspires me and infuses me with hope and optimism."

Steve Fischbein, geologist, wrote "Take a breath, remember what I am doing and why, and then put my head down and kick some serious butt!"

Joann Grosh, RN, MA, executive director of senior services at a large hospital system explained, "I stay away from negative people and call or spend time with people who are positive, fun to be with, have a lot of energy, and are forward thinkers. One friend in particular always makes me laugh and another friend helps me keep my perspective."

As you can see, there are many ways to keep yourself moving forward when times get rough. They include solitary activities that bring you a sense of peace or re-connect you to your passion and purpose, and activities with valued choir members that help you feel refreshed, refueled, and refocused. The key is to determine which activities you like and need, and then commit to doing them regularly.

The bottom line is this: You are important. What you are here to do or create is important. So do whatever you need to do, regularly and consistently, to keep the flame of your passion alive and dancing so you can persevere in the name of the song in you.

PICK AN ACCOUNTABILITY PARTNER

You don't, of course, have to keep the flame in you burning all by your lonesome. Having someone besides your sweet self to talk to, someone who can help you stay psyched up and centered on your journey from here to there, is of tremendous value. Speaking for myself, I can't begin to tell you how helpful it is to have what I call an accountability partner—a choir member I respect and value who helps me hold to what I have said I want to achieve or create. Over the years, those partners have included teachers, mentors, life coaches, and business coaches. As a professional coach, I value the act and the art of coaching. I've already mentioned my business coach, Mark Le Blanc. He gently (and, when needed, not so gently) keeps me moving forward. He, has, for example played a big part in helping me shape and finish this book in a timely manner. Having my own coach helps keep me on track, even and especially when I am going through a rough patch (which, of course, invariably happens to everyone from time to time).

Would a coach work for you? Or, if not a coach, how about the consistent counsel of a wise friend or mentor? Consider creating a simple contract spelling out what you intend to do and by when, and then having your friend or mentor sign it as your accountability partner. It is remarkable how words on paper, and the witness and encouragement of a genuine choir member, can keep you from bailing on your goal.

THE MAGIC OF MASTERMINDS

Here's another option for establishing accountability and forward movement through thick or thin. Create or join a mastermind group—a small group of like-minded business choir members you meet with regularly in person, by phone, or via video conferencing. During your meetings, you take turns brainstorming, clarifying, and setting specific action steps that will help you move towards your individual goals. At the next mastermind meeting—say, a month later—you hold each other accountable for having done what you said you were going to do to achieve your goals. Then you start the process all over again, defining and declaring what you intend to accomplish by your next scheduled mastermind meeting.

Here's how Shelley Fitzgerald, creative artist, certified health educator, and the head and heart of Everything Fitz, describes the choir member/mastermind based system of accountability that works for her:

"The first step is properly identifying the goal that aligns with my greater vision based on serving others and walking in love. Second is to share the goal with a friend or supportive circle of friends and/or colleagues who can hold me accountable and lift me up when necessary. Lastly, I focus on feeding my body, mind, and soul daily the best I can to be able to work at optimal performance in moving through the steps."

Creating and maintaining a system of personal accountability that works for you is key to helping yourself move forward through challenges. Whether you hire a coach, reach out regularly to a close choir member, or create a mastermind group, make sure the relationship or the system you choose is something you like that you will actually do.

So find someone—or a group of someones—you can meet with regularly, who can keep you honest about the progress you're making towards your goals. Nothing will kick your butt and make you want to take action more than having to 'fess up to someone else.

JUST DO IT!

Ultimately, perseverance is about taking persistent, consistent action, no matter what—even if the only action you can manage in this moment, on this day, is one teeny, tiny little thing. Without energized action, there is no forward movement. As any runner at the starting line will tell you.

When you find yourself struggling to take a specific action step towards advancing your passion and purpose, ask yourself, "If I don't take this step, will I someday wish I had?" If your answer is yes, take a breath, ratchet up your will, and do everything in your power to take that action step. As the keeper of the song in you, you are, after all, responsible for its development. That means committing to taking steps forward, even when it might be easier not to. Not taking regular, consistent action on behalf of the song in you ultimately leads to a trip to Bittertown, where you wallow in sadness and regret.

As social media guru Emily Hay eloquently explains, "My regret for *not* doing something, for *not* trying, for *not* pushing, for *not* satisfying my appetite to try to succeed is *far worse* than the regret I would face never having tried at all. I say, 'it's better to have taken action towards achieving one's dream than never to have acted at all.'"

So today, just do one thing.

And then another.

And another.

You won't regret it.

SAY "AAA"
On a separate piece of paper, answer the following questions and complete the following exercises:

ATTITUDE
- What is your general attitude about perseverance or taking persistent action? What do you tend to think, believe, or do when needing to persevere when the challenges mount?

- What affirmation can you create, repeat, and embrace to maintain a more positive attitude towards taking persistent action (e.g., "I move forward with purpose and determination.")?

ACTION

1. When faced with an avalanche of no's, what are the top three things you do to help move yourself or your business forward?

2. If a friend or colleague struggling with a setback came to you for advice on how to get unstuck and move forward, what suggestions would you give him or her?

3. What activities fan the flame of passion and purpose in you? What do you need and love to be around, or do, to lift your spirit, reactivate your enthusiasm, or re-energize your body?

4. Grab a choir member and have him or her record you while you tell why you are the perfect person to be pursuing your passion and purpose. Go into detail, and let your enthusiasm soar. Listen to the recording regularly, especially when you need a boost.

5. What *one* action step are you willing to take this week to encourage yourself to move forward with persistence?

ACCOUNTABILITY

What will you do/what system of accountability will you put into place to help yourself complete this week's action step?

CHAPTER TWELVE

The Gift of Self Direction

"Angel on my shoulder, sing your music through me.
Angel on my shoulder, sing me sweet melody."
—ELENI KELAKOS, "ANGEL ON MY SHOULDER," *I WILL FLY*

"Home is a place inside us, home is the flame that guides us
Love is what fuels the flame, and life is change
And change is who you are—be your own North Star."
—ELENI KELAKOS, "CHANGE," *TOUCH THE SKY*

"Maybe you should create your own show? Something to showcase yourself and help other people figure out how to cast you…"

I don't remember who said those words. I do remember shrugging them off. Because I still clutched so hard to the fairytale wish that someone else would create the perfect project for me, and invite me to star in it.

But those words must have had Velcro on their undersides, because they stuck to me no matter how hard I tried to brush them off.

The notion of writing my own, one-woman show was planted like a wayward seed that takes root with determination between the hard, gray squares of a city sidewalk.

"What if," I started to muse, "what if..."

The little seed began to shiver and grow, poking tiny tendrils into my con-sciousness, usually when I was just settling down to sleep.

"What if... I created a one woman show... a show about a narcissistic diva whose career is on the skids? A larger than life character, with boobs out to here, fingernails *that* long, false eyelashes like butterfly wings, and a ribald sense of humor? A diva whose publicist suggests she put on a special show for her adoring—but swiftly diminishing—fans at which she can promote her new diva workout video? What if...?"

The little voice in me, the one that, so long ago, had whispered, "Could be more. You could sing for the world," now nagged me incessantly: "Write the diva show! Write the diva show!"

And so, one evening, after dinner, without any fanfare, without anyone but me pushing me to do it, I pulled out my trusty old college typewriter and started writing.

It came easily, this bubbly mélange of text and songs I dubbed *Diva's World*. So utterly thrilled by the presence of a finished product, squalling like a newborn on my kitchen table, I barely registered the little effort there was to its delivery.

Now that I had written it, where was I going to perform it? I turned to my college friend Rusty McGee, who had played Sancho to my Aldonza in *Man of La Mancha*. Rusty was managing the West Bank Café, an intimate perfor-mance space that seemed just right for what appeared to be a mixture of cabaret and performance art. He generously green-lighted a three-day run of *Diva's World* at the theatre, and I launched into rehearsals. My husband, Marcus, took on the role of director. I sent out a handwritten invitation to my mailing list that read like this.

Darlings!

Come witness the premiere of *Diva's World*, my very own, very Diva, very delicious talk show! Come to the West Bank and let me tempt you with morsels from the Diva Handbook, my definitive how-to guide for the budding Diva!

I guarantee fun, frolic, and a surefire way to have *fabulous* nails.

XXX's
Diva

It's opening night at the West Bank Cafe, and the place is packed to the rafters.

I am padded out to there, fake boobs in triple D territory. Stuffed into a satin fuchsia cocktail dress, I bat my enormously fake eyelashes, pat my overly poufed hair, and shake both my rhinestone earrings and my booty as I totter onto the small stage in skyscraper heels. Larger that life? Hell, yes! I am the diva, and this is Diva's World. I gesture to the pianist, and begin to sing my intentionally hokey theme song, "Diva's world, diva's world…"

Amazingly, the audience leaps into the silliness from the get-go, willing to go right along with me on this giddy, wild ride. I sing longingly about my fictional sugar daddy, Orville Redenbacher, the popcorn maven, while passing around a large bowl of popcorn. I educate the audience on the characteristics of true budding divas, showing them slides of me as a child sipping champagne out of a paper cup and carrying a bouquet of roses. Finally, I demonstrate the diva workout. This involves doing calisthenics and aerobic moves using four workout tools that represent the quintessential diva: One is a fluffy, fuchsia, feather boa, which I use as a jump rope. The remaining three are oversized cloth body parts I've stitched, stuffed and decorated, and which I toss, juggle and bench press with the help of my emcee. They include a huge eyeball with massive, quivering lashes, an oversized hand with extremely long and vibrant nails, and the satin-clad torso of a woman with a glitzy necklace and shockingly large boobs. The audience hollers and screams. And I have the time of my life, sharing this thing I've created, this thing that is mine.

When I'm done, a director whom I greatly respect pulls me aside and says, "Writing your own material is the answer."

Remarkably, I ignored that truth for almost three more years.

CALIFORNIA, HERE I COME

It was inevitable: What actor worth his or her salt wouldn't eventually want to test the waters of Hollywood—especially when the opportunities in New York seemed increasingly limited? Following the lead of so many of our actor colleagues, my husband and I sublet our co-op apartment, packed our bags, and relocated to Los Angeles, hoping for the usual—fame, fortune, and, in our case, perhaps a new lease on life for what was clearly a marriage in trouble.

I loved California. It reminded me of Israel, with its hot, desert weather, azure ocean, and emphasis on outdoor living. Marcus and I moved into a cute rental house in the San Fernando Valley, close to the freeways we would travel to our respective auditions. After eight years of riding public transportation in New York City, I learned to drive all over again, stalling out my car countless times as I maneuvered the stick shift through Hollywood's canyons and hills. It was a heady time, learning the do's and don'ts of a very different kind of entertainment industry than I'd experienced in Manhattan.

Maybe the move forced the issue, but it didn't take much more than a year after our move West for the underpinnings of my marriage to unravel completely. I'll spare you the details. What's important to note is that, when I moved out, I took my guitar and my piano to my new apartment. The last time I'd actually played my guitar had been to serenade some elderly nursing home residents through New York's Hospital Audiences, Inc. program two years before. But in my new circumstances, taking my instruments with me—along with my journals, my first computer, and some precious family pictures—seemed not only comforting but imperative.

Defining and developing my new life, I found myself drawn to new choir members, friends who enriched and supported me.

One of them was a handsome and brilliant actor, Thor Edgell, who would eventually become my second husband. The other was a warm, funny and stunningly talented singer and actress named Lisa Michelson. Lisa became my new best friend almost as soon as we met at a seminar held by a Hollywood casting director. We sang together, conspired to write a play, and talked incessantly over fat California artichokes, white wine, and cappuccinos. Lisa told me about the positive results of her pregnancy test even before she told her husband, Greg. And she was the first person I bared my soul to about Marcus and my choice to leave him.

It was to Lisa's home that my mother, who was visiting from Boston, Thor, and I drove for dinner on a night that would change the course of my life.

ANGEL ON MY SHOULDER

The dogs were home, the door was open, but where was Lisa? Or Greg?

Ma, Thor, and I stood in Lisa's strangely silent house, wondering if Lisa, in her hormonally charged state, had somehow flaked and forgotten her plans to have us over for dinner.

We barely noticed Greg's little red sports car parked at an awkward angle in the street outside their house. And we certainly didn't notice the fresh dent in the passenger side. If we had, perhaps I wouldn't have been as shocked when, near midnight, Greg called to deliver the news that they'd been in an accident and Lisa was dead, killed by a driver who'd ignored a traffic light.

Lisa was three months pregnant and only thirty-one years young—my age—when that accident took her life. Sobering, to say the least; in some ways, even more so than my father's death, which had occurred only seven months

earlier. Daddy's loss had been expected: He was seventy-eight, and had suf-

earlier. Daddy's loss had been expected: He was seventy-eight, and had suffered from Parkinson's for almost twenty years. But the force of nature that was Lisa had her whole life ahead of her. And her death was devastating.

One loss after another—my marriage, my father, my friend. It was almost too much to bear.

Turning to my old pal—music—for comfort, I began to noodle around on my guitar, hack around on my piano. On impulse, I recorded a snatch of a tune I was fiddling with as the outgoing message on my answering machine. Remarkably, everyone who called mentioned how much they liked it. Mary, the dear, frail, elderly landlord from whom I rented my apartment, kept calling, "Just to hear your lovely voice, dear." These affirmations stirred me into reaching more and more for my instruments.

One morning I woke up with a melody in my head, along with what appeared to be a complete set of lyrics. I stumbled over to the piano and composed a song, from soup to nuts, in about half an hour. It was about Lisa Michelson, and it was called "Angel on My Shoulder".

The song wrote itself. I just got out of the way.

"Angel on my shoulder, speak your music through me.
Angel on my shoulder, sing me sweet melody."

I knew—just knew—that Lisa was speaking through me. And that she wanted me to keep her spirit alive through the music that was starting to bubble up— strong and insistent—from my deepest self.

I remembered what my friend the director had said to me after seeing *Diva's World*, three years before, "Writing your own material is the answer." He was right.

Song after song poured out of me. I reached out and captured them, on scraps of paper, kitchen towels, cassette tape. I was suddenly on a mission to express thoughts, feelings, opinions, and needs I had kept buried for years. The cosmic clues were clearly pointing me in the direction of music—*my* music.

I had something to say. Who knew?

A DEFINING DECLARATION

My apartment complex is burning all around me.
But I am safe, in a clearing in the middle.
I am not afraid.
A strange, gnome-like being trots up to me.
"Would you like me to get your things from your apartment?"
I nod.
He sprints away.
When he returns, he is carrying a collection of items, but not the ones I want to see.
"Where is my guitar?" I ask "Where are my songs?"
"I didn't know you needed them," the gnome shrugs.
"Don't you understand?" I reply, "My music is my life's work!"

And then I was awake, sitting bolt upright in bed. The dream I'd just had was as clear and radiant as the sun streaming through my window.

"My music is my life's work!"

Holy cow!! I had just declared myself.

Suddenly, nothing—not even my acting career—seemed more important than writing my songs and sharing them with others. The songs were stalking me at every turn and coming so fast it was all I could do keep up with them. Some of them were even starting to sound pretty good. Thor shook his head when he heard me singing my new tunes. "How do you do this?" he asked. "It's such a gift."

I timidly shared my songs with a friend who had a recording studio in his basement, thinking, for some reason, that maybe I ought to make a demo. I sat at his piano and played and sang one song, and then another. When I turned, I saw that my friend was in tears.

"You could do this professionally," he declared. Another cosmic clue.

When I played my new songs for my good friend Joe, he surprised me by getting mad. Practically shaking me by the shoulders, he asked, "Why haven't you been sharing these songs with the public?" I had no adequate reply. "For God's sake," Joe said, rolling his eyes, "get off your butt and go sing at an open mic talent night!"

And so I did. Not just to get Joe off my back, but to satisfy the inner voice in me that was at it again, hissing, "You could sing for the world," nudging me (and my songs) firmly up and out of the basement. I threw my hat in the lottery to sing at the weekly open mic night at Highland Grounds coffeehouse in Hollywood. And when my name was called; when I stood on the stage, cradling my guitar, my cosmic goosebumps the size of golf balls; when my voice seemed to grab and hush the chattering audience; when, after my final strum, the hoots, hollers, and applause washed over me; and when, like the cherry on top, the owner of the coffeehouse offered me a paying gig on the spot, I knew I was on to something.

And all because I stepped out of the basement and shared my song.

STUDIO MAGIC

The Los Angeles acoustic music community opened its arms to me with alacrity. And as it did, I attracted new choir members, people meant to help me define my voice and bring my songs to a larger audience.

The first was Dr. Jeffrey Laham, an insightful, visionary psychologist. Jeff bluntly called me out on my tendency towards being a parts car, and encouraged me to commit to my development as both an artist and as a strong, actualized woman. He was a monumental champion of the songs I penned, celebrating each one as they arrived, like bawling babies, into the world.

The second was Sanda Jasper, the profoundly intuitive spiritual counselor and life coach I mentioned in the previous chapter. Sanda schooled me in the power of the mind and the intention to create my reality—tools I use to this day with my own clients. At our first meeting, Sanda told me she saw music all around me, and that it was important I share it with people—especially women—around the world. This was before I had even discussed my song-writing with her. Cosmic goosebumps? Oh yes!

The third was Doug Messenger, a gifted producer and sound engineer. From the get-go, it was clear that Doug and I shared a similar sense of life, musical vision, and penchant for excellence. When I told Doug I wanted to record a demo of my songs, he came at me with one better. Why not record an entire album at his recording studio? Because I intuitively and absolutely knew Doug was the right musical partner for me, and that my songs would be in good hands with him as producer and engineer, I was all-in. As if by miracle, the money to produce an album found its way to me; as did an assortment of talented musicians eager to help me take my songs to their highest level. With all the necessary elements in place, Doug and I began to record eleven songs, determined to make studio magic.

I am standing in the control room of Doug Messenger's studio, watching through the glass partition as the members of a professional, thirteen-piece string section get ready to record the string parts for "I Will Fly," the title song of my album. I'd written this song in defiance of a Nashville producer who had passed on another song of mine because it "didn't fit the Nashville mold." The lyrics and the music to "I Will Fly" had come quickly and fiercely.

"I will break the mold
Color over lines.
I will overflow,
Walk a path that's mine.

I will rise above,
I will fill the sky,
I will, I will fly.

Don't tell me what I cannot do, I will still try.
Don't try to make me into you, I am, I am I."

Doug punches the green recording light. The conductor, Jennifer Russell,—
who has composed the transcendent string arrangements— raises her baton.
Bows are lifted, and cello, violin, and viola come to magnificent life. And the
song that originated from the kernel of an idea deep in my soul is transformed,
captured on tape in its fully formed majesty. Astonished, I am overcome by
gratitude and tears.

In this moment, I know. The song in me is the music I write and sing. I have
found my voice—not by looking outside for it, but by seeking it from within
myself. I am my own North Star: What I know and what I need is always within
reach—if I am willing to listen to and follow the little voice that guides me.

POINTS TO PONDER

Dr. Sherene McHenry, a speaking colleague and human relations expert,
and the author of Pick: *Choose to Create a Life You Love,* explained to me the
essential difference between the way men and women shift into their power.
For men, this passage occurs when they learn to take care of themselves—
and others—from a financial standpoint. For a woman, however, it happens
when she finds her voice.

I get that. As this book attests, not only have I been through the years-long
process of finding and defining my own voice, I am continuously helping and
observing my coaching clients find and define theirs. There is nothing more
exciting than the moment a coaching client realizes and stands in their power
for the first time, free from the fears, hesitations, and anxieties that have
limited them. I have witnessed people embrace who they are and what they
are here to do (on or off the speaking platform) with a sudden, fierce zeal

that is downright mind-blowing. One coaching client I'll call Serena immediately comes to mind:

Serena, an educated and capable professional, had grown up in a culture
that didn't allow much room for women to express or assert themselves. In
spite of this background, she'd demonstrated drive and business savvy, making her the best choice to take over as CEO of the family business. Serena
struggled to find and express her voice as a woman in a position of leadership. It was impossible not to notice that she kept her voice very small and
her passions capped. Until the day she completed and delivered a simple
speaking assignment: Write and deliver a three-to five-minute presentation
about something she was passionate about. Serena stood on my studio stage,
planted her feet, and in a deep, resonant, and animated voice, spoke passionately about being an American in a country that has freedoms for all, irrespec-
tive of their divergent opinions or beliefs. I was stunned. The Serena speaking
in front of me was confident and resolute, with a voice that came from her
belly and bounced off the back walls of my office. She spoke without the
usual questioning lift at the end of her sentences (that would imply the need
for affirmation from her listener). She spoke without the usual qualifiers—
"I think" or "I guess" (that would imply insecurity or lack of commitment).
Serena spoke with such deep conviction and was fueled so passionately by
her inner guidance and knowing, that I was moved to tears. She was just
as surprised—and delighted—as I at the new voice that emerged—a voice
filled with authority, determination and purpose, the voice of a leader.

As Serena realized, helping people hear you and take your wisdom seriously
is an essential part of sharing your voice effectively, especially in a business
setting. In my experience, women have a particularly difficult time giving
themselves permission to express themselves with clarity, conviction, and
confidence. They make their voices small, and walk, sit, and stand in ways
that rob them of their authority. Which is why, when I present my "Stop
Playing Small" program for women in the business world, I share techniques
that will help them be seen and heard with more power and conviction.
Five of the most essential suggestions are:

1. Stop talking like a Valley Girl, letting your voice swoop up like a question mark at the end of your sentence. Instead, speak in strong declarative sentences.

2. Stop apologizing for every little thing, especially something you didn't do.

3. Stop being afraid to toot your own horn. If you don't speak up for yourself, and for your accomplishments, who will?

4. Stop stooping, shrinking, and hiding. Instead, stand and act like a queen: Plant your feet, stand up straight, uncross your arms, and look people in the eye.

5. Stop talking in circles. Get to the point, stick to the point (the men in your life will thank you for this).

Whether you are a man or a woman, you have the power—and the physical instrument—to help others see, feel, and hear your wisdom, your expertise, and your authority. Use it fully and well.

THE BIG HOOK

Finding—and ultimately committing to—one's unique voice can occur both literally (discovering and using a more commanding vocal sound and tone), and metaphorically (finding one's individual form of expression in the world). I see examples of the latter daily in my Blue Sky life coaching practice. Women reach out to me with a longing to express something they can't quite name, but they know is there. It's exciting as heck to watch them begin to trust their own inner knowing as it guides them to discover (or re-discover) what they are meant to do and be in their allotted time on Planet Earth.

Take, for example, my friend Beth, a successful real estate agent. Beth began to scratch her longing to make art by taking oil painting classes. Suddenly, she couldn't get enough of the paint and canvas that seemed to bewitch her. When I visited Beth and her husband several years ago, her paintings had taken over their little den. Beth was clearly on fire with the art that was flowing out of her. Just recently, I received a beautiful postcard inviting me to an exhibit of her works at a local gallery. Beth's art—and her voice—have now spread beyond the walls of her home to the living rooms of other lucky souls who are enjoying its presence on their own walls.

Another example is that of my neighbor Sheryl, a medical doctor with a twenty-year career as an internist. One summer, Sheryl confided in me that her life was going to change radically for the better part of a year. She was leaving her medical practice and moving from Michigan to Ohio to complete a fellowship training program in hospice and palliative medicine. During her absence, her husband would be left behind to tend to their home and her beloved garden.

When I asked Sheryl to explain how her decision to shift from curative medicine to palliative medicine had come about, she explained that she had been through a really trying, eye-opening experience watching beloved family members struggle with end-of-life issues, including her father who was diagnosed with stage four lung cancer. As a daughter, and as a medical practitioner, Sheryl was disappointed and disillusioned by the impersonal and insensitive way her father was treated by the medical professionals who attended him. In an effort to extend his life, her father was put through procedures that served only to increase his discomfort and reduce his dignity. At a particularly difficult moment, when her dad was experiencing uncontrolled pain and his doctors were slow to provide the pain medication he needed, Sheryl finally took the step that would ultimately change her life. She called hospice care, which focuses not on curing a patient, but on giving them comfort and pain relief. Sheryl watched as the emergency hospice nurse tenderly and thoughtfully did her best to alleviate her father's pain. Palliative care brought a greater degree of peace, connection, and closure to Sheryl's father (and to Sheryl and her family members) during his final hours.

The world of difference that hospice and comfort care provided profoundly impacted Sheryl. She wondered, "Is there some way I could contribute in a positive light to people's end-of-life experience that makes a difference to humanity?" That thought sat on the shelf for a couple of months, until her elderly mother-in-law broke her hip. At the hospital, while sitting at her mother-in-laws's bedside, Sheryl had a spirited conversation with a visiting chaplain about the trend toward aggressiveness in heath care practices, and her budding interest in comfort care for elderly and end-of-life patients. The chaplain heartily suggested that Sheryl meet the hospital's palliative care physician, Dr. Craig. By sheer coincidence, Dr. Craig was standing in the hall-way when Sheryl accompanied the chaplain out of her mother-in-law's room. The chaplain introduced Sheryl to the doctor. Their ensuing conversations kicked off Sheryl's decision to willingly disrupt her life, move to Ohio, and complete a year-long fellowship training in hospice and palliative medicine. When Sheryl described the defining moment that propelled her to make this life-changing decision, she simply said, "I just knew. A light bulb went off. I had an intense, physical sensation of being pulled, right in the center of my bra strap, yanking me forward. I realized, 'Oh my gosh, I'm being called!' Like some presence and life force said 'this is what I need you for!'"

A year afterward, with the often grueling training under her belt, and her board certification only a few months away, Sheryl accepted a brand new position at a nearby hospital as an inpatient palliative medicine consultant. Not only that, she worked under Dr. Craig, the very physician who had urged her to move forward on realizing her dream. And she has never been happier.

As you can see by Sheryl's experience, once your path of expression reveals itself to you, it's often near to impossible to ignore it. Which is why Beth started painting and couldn't (or wouldn't) stop. Or why Sheryl felt so com-pelled to turn her life upside down for the sake of a left turn in her life's path.

What's important to notice about both Sheryl and Beth, is that instead of looking outside of themselves for affirmation, feedback, guidance, or permis-sion, they trusted their own innate wisdom, the pull of their own inner voice. They listened to themselves. And then they just went for it.

MAKE THE SPACE FOR GRACE

In her memoir, *A Woman of Egypt*, Jehan Sadat, wife of Egyptian President
Anwar Sadat, describes how her husband often retreated by himself to the
garden of a government residence called The Barrage Rest Home when he
needed to make an important decision or contemplate a specific action.
Located outside the city, and away from the crowds and the noise, the
garden offered President Sadat a peaceful setting in which to meditate and
gain perspective on a pressing problem. He stayed in the garden as long as
he needed—sometimes days in a row—to work through the issue at hand.[9]
President Sadat understood the value of taking time to get quiet and go deep
so he could tap into his internal wisdom. He made the space for grace.

When it comes to making space for grace so he can make the tough decisions
that affect his business, my husband, Jim, the Chairman of a music talent
agency, has developed an approach similar to President Sadat's. First, he
invites the counsel of key people in his organization and listens carefully to
their analysis of the issue at hand, their opinions, and their recommendations.
Then he comes home and retreats to the bathroom, where he runs a bath,
complete with fragrant oils. Then, with classical or new age music wafting
in the background, he soaks in the soothing water and meditates on the
problem he needs to solve. In the privacy of the bathroom, Jim sits and soaks
and thinks for however long he needs to come to a final decision. In the
end, it is his own counsel he heeds. Once he makes his decision, he never
questions it.

I am continuously struck by Jim's rock-solid ability to trust in his own wisdom.
He owns his decisions and stands by them. And he has developed a process—
meditating in the bathtub—that allows him the time and the stillness to turn
his attention within so he can access his inner wisdom.

Like Jim, or President Sadat, you have the ability to listen to your own inner
wisdom and act on what you know is right for you, without looking for affirmation or confirmation from others. Take the time you need to connect with
your deep knowing, and to embrace a process—meditation; solitary walks;

musings in your journal; prayer; yoga—that allows you to stop, get quiet and listen in. Once you've accessed what you need to know, you can then rejoin the greater world, sharing your voice and your wisdom with confidence and authority.

WHAT'S OLD IS NEW

When you brush up against a passion that's hooked into your soul role, it feels at once familiar and compelling —it's like a potential lover you can't get out of your system. Every time you get near it, you feel more alive. And while you may have spent some time before, nudging up to your passion, all of a sudden you want to do more than just flirt with it. You want to romance it, wake up at dawn with it, and devote your heart to it. Because, suddenly, the little voice inside you is not only adamant, it's crystal clear. "Time to commit!" it says. "Time to move forward!"

When that moment comes, when the cosmic clues shine a light on a talent, a passion, or a cause that seems familiar yet new, and so strangely compelling to you that you can't and won't stop doing it, hanging around it, or thinking about it, no matter what anybody says, pay attention. Trust that you are recognizing cosmic clues essential to your personal expression and development. And then leap with gusto into singing the song you were meant to sing.

That's what I did when I committed to my songwriting (or any other vital manifestation of my passion and purpose): Instead of waiting for someone else to hand me what I needed and wanted, I took action and generated it myself.

Nobody knows what's best for you better than you. And no one is going to be more passionate about making it a reality than you. Not your parents, not your spouse, not your siblings, not your teachers, not your best friend. You, alone, are privy to the little voice in you, the inner wisdom that gives you your marching orders and feeds your unique voice and your individual expression.

So be your own North Star.

Fill your own need.

Trust that you have the power to guide yourself exactly where you want to go.

SAY "AAA"

On a piece of paper, answer the following questions and complete the suggested exercises:

ATTITUDE

• What is your general attitude about trusting your inner guidance? What do you tend to think, believe, or do about being self-directed?

• What affirmation can you create, repeat, and embrace to maintain a more positive attitude towards trusting your inner wisdom (e.g., "I trust in the wisdom that guides me.")?

ACTION

1. What are the personal mantras you tend to use to help yourself feel more centered and calm (e.g., "I am safe, I am loved," or "All is well.")?

2. What do you regularly do to help yourself still the mind, get quiet, and go deep, so you can access the little voice inside that guides you? What practices—yoga, t'ai chi, prayer, journaling, etc.—do you regularly turn to? What practices could you add to your life to help you access your inner voice?

3. Describe a time or circumstance when you acted upon a strong inner knowing that resulted in a positive outcome. How did trusting your own voice and intuition make you feel?

4. Create your own wisdom cards: Rather than buy a deck of inspirational cards featuring other people's wise or inspirational sayings, create your own. Write down everything you know for sure—the guiding principles of your life—in simple sentences (e.g., "To learn how to meditate, watch a cat."). Then transfer your wise sayings to small, blank cards. Decorate the cards with paint, pictures, or drawings. Refer to them (and to your own innate wisdom) on a daily basis.

5. What *one* action step are you willing to take this week to encourage yourself to listen to and be guided by your inner voice?

ACCOUNTABILITY

What will you do/what system of accountability will you put into place to help yourself complete this week's action step?

CHAPTER THIRTEEN

The Gift of Surrender

"Smiling, alive, arms open wide,
Into the Wild Why Not..."
—GREG GREENWAY, "INTO THE WILD WHY NOT," *FROM MUSSOLINI'S HEAD*

"It's huge when you embrace the life you didn't plan on."
—Greenberg[10]

"And change is who you are.
Be your own North Star."
—Eleni Kelakos, "Change," from *Touch the Sky*

SAINT PATRICK'S DAY, 1998

I am forty years and thirteen days old.
A peaceful morning. Still in my pajamas, I stand in the office of my apartment,
watching with amusement as Thor, my husband of four years, gingerly tries out
our brand new Sony computer. The vivid color screen—our first—is as bewitch-
ing as a summer butterfly.

Absorbed, we're taken aback by a sudden explosion—BAM! The monitor screen
goes black. Every light in the house fizzles to darkness. What the hell?

For a moment, we wonder, Did Thor hit the wrong button? Did the guys working on the bridge outside our apartment hit a power line?

Then, the smell of smoke, and we are on full alert, seeking its source. In the kitchen, we gasp at the sight: Fingers of dense smoke surge with malicious intent through the heating vents. Fire in the basement!

Racing out the front door, we find our downstairs neighbor training a garden hose on flames shooting out of the electrical box on the side of the building. "Call the fire department," he screams. The stream from the garden hose looks tiny and useless against the lashing flames.

We run back into our apartment. "Get the cat," I holler, "I'll make the call!" Thor heads for the bedroom, where Cassie, our two-year-old tortoiseshell, has scooted in a scared crouch under the king-sized bed. I grab for the phone. No electricity! No dial tone! And it would be two years before I would own a cell phone. We're screwed unless I get to a functioning phone.

On the way back out the front door, I instinctively grab my guitar and the hard copies of my music. I can't, however, carry the four large boxes of newly minted CDs—two thousand copies of I Will Fly, delivered just yesterday—stacked and vulnerable in my music studio.

I place my guitar and sheet music carefully on the lawn and run to find a neighbor with a working phone. I bang on the door of one house after another, screaming, "Fire, fire, help, help!" But at 11:00 a.m. on Saint Patrick's Day, either no one is home or no one is answering.

Precious moments wing by as the fire gobbles up my home. Following the sounds of hammering, I stumble onto three workmen laying scaffolding against a nearby house. Though they speak mostly Spanish, they understand the wild look in my eyes and the words "fire," "help," and "call 911" I yell over and over again. "I call," a workman assures me.

I race back to my burning apartment. It's now filled with black smoke, and Thor is still inside, trying to fish Cassie out from under the bed.

*"Leave her!" I scream, my heart cleaving at the words. "Get out! Get out!"
Sobbing, we run from the building, just as four fire engines tear up the street,
sirens blaring.*

But it's too late.

By the time they can contain the fire, the damage is done.

Twenty minutes later, we stand stunned at our losses:

*Our beloved cat, overcome by the smoke in spite of the firemen's attempt to
revive her.*

Half of our belongings, incinerated by flame or blackened by smoke.

*The beautiful, affordable spacious home we love, the stucco gem from 1926 about
which I have recently declared, "It would take an act of God to make me leave
this apartment," rendered uninhabitable.*

We are uninsured. And we are homeless.

But we are alive.

*And the four big boxes of my brand new I Will Fly CDs sitting in the music room
of our burned-out home? Utterly unscathed. A small miracle that ignites a scat-
tering of Cosmic Goosebumps across my skin. Hope amid the smoldering ruins.*

OUT OF THE ASHES

It's true what they say about shock. When you're in it, you are numb from
the inside out.

After the fire, we were in shock for days, probably months.

Homeless and in mourning—for our cat and for the feeling of safety and security that had been suddenly ripped away—I had never felt so vulnerable, so unmoored. There was nothing to do but surrender to exactly what was happening and trust that it was meant to be, even if it was completely unexpected and not part of my plan. Nothing to do but leap "Into the Wild Why Not," as singer and songwriter, Greg Greenway, so ably put it.

I had to believe that everything was happening for a reason, even the bad stuff. There was a silver lining somewhere, if I was willing to look for it.

Actually, the silver lining was easy to spot: It shone from the faces of my loving, smiling, and concerned friends and choir members—and even total strangers—who rallied around to help us recover from our catastrophe.

The children at the bilingual elementary school next door from our now boarded-up apartment presented us with a massive card with a hand-drawn picture of Cassie and their heartfelt thoughts scrawled in crayon: "I am sorry your cat died," one child wrote. "I lost my Gramma last year. I was sad. I hope you get a new cat!"

People we'd never met, who'd read about us in the newspaper or seen the fire on TV, showed up to help us find our cat (they mistakenly thought she was still alive) or to reassure us that we would find another cat someday and love it with abandon. Others sent us money, brought us bags of food, gave us gift cards to The Gap so we could replace our clothing. The outpouring of love and support was incredible.

But my choir members went above and beyond anything I could have imagined:

Stephanie—the first on the scene—helped us bury Cassie, held me while I sobbed, and took huge piles of soiled clothes to the dry cleaner.

Brenda took us into her home the first night, tucking us into bed like children. For the next week, she quietly washed mountains of smoke smeared laundry while we shivered, cried and slept.

After the first week was up, Brigitte took us into her home folding us—and my mom, who had flown in from Massachusetts—into her arms like we were family.

Steve, a dear friend who had, himself, been through a horrific fire that destroyed his home, his thousand-dollar Canali suits, his gold convertible, and his sense of security, approached us on a day when various choir members joined forces to help us pull out and clean the last remaining articles from our condemned apartment. The stench of smoke clung to everything, and Steve, hating the memories it evoked, kept his distance. He pulled me to a seated position on my neighbor's stoop, and handed me three, crisp hundred-dollar bills. "There will come a time," he said, "when you will be sick to death of staying on people's couches and are longing for privacy. Please use this money to stay a night at a fabulous hotel so you can remind yourself that there is more than the strange limbo you're experiencing."

I kept that money in a safe place, determined to use it the way Steve suggested. I had no idea that those three, crisp, green bills, would, like the fire, serve to flip the switch that would, metaphorically speaking, move the train I was riding to a brand new track.

WHEN FIRE HEALS

After a month of searching, we found a tiny, but bewitching, Spanish style house with a fat palm tree in the front yard. My mom helped us finish cleaning, sorting, and putting away the last of our belongings, and then flew back home to Massachusetts.

Left alone, without my mother and the phalanx of choir members who'd been propping us up for the better part of a month, Thor and I slid messily between tears, joy at being alive, and a kind of grudging resignation at our newly configured reality.

"Why did this happen?" I wondered, endlessly. Things had been ticking along so nicely: We'd been so happy in our large and lovely home. Our beloved kitten had joyously grown into healthy adulthood, and my career as a singer, songwriter and recording artist had just started to solidify. Why, then, would we have to have the rug pulled out from under us by a freak fire caused by rainwater pooling on the roof and leaking into the electrical conduit? Why did things always have to change, so often and so much?

Over time, I began to understand that the fire, and all its positive and negative ramifications, was designed to teach me a key life lesson: That change happens just when you least expect it; and that letting go and leaning into the moment— no matter what the moment presented—is the key to living a conscious and purposeful life.

 As a control freak, learning how to let go and dive "Smiling, alive, arms open wide into the Wild Why Not," as my singer-songwriter pal Greg so niftily puts it, was—and still is—my hardest lesson. But I was determined to try.

In that unraveled but receptive state of mind, I chanced upon a flyer for a Celebrate Life Retreat being held at the Ojai Foundation in the Santa Barbara foothills. The little voice in me was surprisingly adamant, "Register for this." And so I did, using, at last, the three hundred dollar bills that Steve had given me.

THE WAY IS SHOWN

The Celebrate Life Retreat was healing and revealing—everything I'd hoped it would be:

Ropes courses had me dangling off of mountainsides or leaping off of sixty-foot trees.

Mind-blowing workshops encouraged me to confront my inner blocks and fears.

Creative exercises allowed me to putter and dream.

A Native American sweat lodge opened my pores and my heart and renewed my sense of possibility.

All on a stunning piece of land dotted by breathtaking pieces of art—a giant Buddha statue looming in a field; colorful weavings hanging like brilliant spider webs in the trees; evocative sculptures gracing winding paths and meeting places.

I was particularly impressed by the spirit, nature, and abilities of the workshop leaders, a loving and dynamic bunch from all walks of the healing world. I connected profoundly and particularly with Richard Hatch, a joyous, loquacious actor and motivational speaker known for playing Captain Apollo in the original *Battlestar Galactica* television series. Richard and I talked frequently and easily throughout the weekend. I had impulsively brought along my guitar, and Richard seemed delighted when I played my song "I Will Fly" to the collected group around a campfire one star-drenched night.

At the end of the weekend, he pulled me aside and said, "You need to get up and speak to groups of people." When I explained that I was already doing that, by way of the songs I was writing and sharing with others, he shook his head. "No," he said, "I'm talking about something different, something more. You're a way-shower," he said, with finality. "I know one when I see one."

"A way-shower!" Those words instantly gave me the cosmic goosebumps. Intuitively, I knew Richard was right. I folded the precious gift of his words into my heart.

When the weekend was over, two things happened in quick succession: The members of the Celebrate Life Foundation, who had created and facilitated the retreat weekend, asked me to both join their board and create a workshop of my own for their next retreat.

I had never led a workshop. But I intuitively felt I could. And so, without much fuss or struggle, I created a workshop that involved using sound and rhythm to encourage self-expression. Facilitating it came surprisingly easily— I was, after all, tapping into all of the tools and techniques I'd learned as an actor. And I discovered I loved helping people move through their fears and into a greater, more conscious, and authentic presence.

At his generous invitation, I joined Richard Hatch on stage a few months later at a metaphysical retreat in Las Vegas where he was speaking. Sharing not only my songs but my thoughts and—dare I say—the wisdom that had been percolating in me for years felt both new and natural. Something stirred deeply in me, not to be ignored. Still more cosmic goosebumps!

And all the while I was writing and singing my songs, building an audience through a succession of tours up and down the length of California that I was booking myself as chief, cook, and bottle washer of EEK! Records. Songs from *I Will Fly* were getting consistent airplay on folk/acoustic radio stations, which was thrilling. Encouraged, I birthed another CD—*To the Bone*, a stripped-down collection of songs that opened up still more opportunities for me. One song from *To the Bone*, "The Tallest Poppy," quickly began to have a life of its own. The song told the story of a little poppy named Petal who—in spite of opposition from other poppies dared to defy the law of the Poppy Land by growing past the Limit sign and taller than the other poppies. In so doing, she encouraged a generation of baby poppies to follow suit, growing to their full potential. Parents and educators loved "The Tallest Poppy," wanting to share it with their kids.

It quickly became apparent to me that "The Tallest Poppy" could inspire people to respect, honor, and develop the song in them—especially girls on the cusp of adolescence, who were moving into the wild and wooly waters of middle school where peer pressure and societal norms would tamp down their inclination to stand out. The cosmic clues were positively screaming about the need to create and present a one-woman show and workshop for girls based on the theme of self-empowerment of "The Tallest Poppy" song. And so, again without a whole lot of muss and fuss, I did. I began booking

"The Tallest Poppy" program in schools, speaking to groups of pre-teens and their moms, but groups nonetheless, just as Richard Hatch had predicted. Step by step, I was being led to speaking—and, more than that—to use my voice to help others heal, face their fears, and manifest their best selves.

Slowly, I was beginning to see the connections between the cosmic clues, the "Aha!" moments that caused me to shift left or right on my path. From actor to singer to songwriter to speaker and workshop leader to advocate for human potential—one thing led to another, if I paid attention, if I followed the cosmic clues. It was just like those follow-the-dots puzzles I'd played as a kid: Follow the dots, link them all together, and the unified picture they created would be revealed.

I now understood that out of chaos comes clarity.

I now understood that I was being shown the way—my way, my path—one cosmic clue at a time, and that I was exactly where I was meant to be on my path.

I now understood that all would be well if I was willing to trust each unfolding moment.

Which is why—when my eight-year marriage to Thor dissolved; when I moved to Boston to care for my ailing mother; when I met Jim, my beloved husband, in a cab at a music conference in Jacksonville, Florida, and moved to Michigan within three months to be by his side, I just went with it, stepping bravely, trustfully into the Wild Why Not.

....

POINTS TO PONDER

The interesting thing about preparing and planning is that life just happens in spite of it. A 6.8 magnitude earthquakes shakes you out of bed at 3:30 in the morning; on a Friday, after school, you're suddenly evacuated from Israel because the Six Day War has begun; a bomb goes off in a house a block away from you in the Gaza Strip; both your parents are smacked to the ground with long-term, debilitating illnesses; you're not ever, ever cast in a Broadway show; not one but two of your marriages quietly unravel; and you wind up living with teenage step-kids in a village of four hundred people in the heart of farmland when you've been an urban girl your whole life.

All those things happened to me, and they were *not*, I assure you, part of the plan.

I don't know how old you are, or what you've experienced in your life thus far. But there is no question in my mind that you've also been surprised at what has popped up to flip you on your rear end along your carefully planned path.

Planning is great. Planning is wonderful. But so is listening to the cosmic clues and letting them help you shape your path all along the way, trusting in their guidance. Sometimes the cosmic clues lead you someplace you least expected to go. And sometimes the cosmic clues appear to you in the most unlikely places: Smack dab in the middle of what appears to be a horrific, life-changing event, like a fire, the death of a loved one, or a debilitating illness.

As I wrote in the song snippet that headlines this chapter, "Change is who you are." Getting comfortable with change is what life is all about. As soon as you think you have it all figured out, something unexpected will throw you for a loop.

I have a friend I'll call Barbara who has been dealing with her aging mother's health issues. It became clear that Barb's mom needed to move into an assisted living facility, where she could be properly taken care of. Barb and her family spent weeks looking for the right place. When they found it, they spent many exhausting hours convincing their mom to move in. After the move, which, in and of itself was stressful, Barb relaxed.

"That's done," she told me. "Mom's all settled."

Well, as my mother used to say, "Famous last words."

A week later (and I can feel you, shaking your head, expecting this), her mom fell and broke her hip. Yep.

The perfect assisted living place and the plan that went along with it instantly became moot. Barb's mom had surgery, while Barb went off looking for a nursing home that, like the hunt for the right assisted living place, took many precious hours. And just when she'd moved her mother into the nursing home, breathing yet another sigh of relief, the rug under Barb's feet shifted again: Funding for her job fell through, and she was laid off.

Change upon change upon change upon change. Ouch!

But Barb is a wise woman with the advantage of many years of insight and experience under her belt.

She picked up a corner of the big, dark cloud of change that threatened her and peeked underneath for the proverbial silver lining. It took a little searching, but there it was, in the form of two profound realizations. The first was that being laid off would allow her to look for a job that would be less exhausting and more fulfilling. The second was the pride and satisfaction she felt from doing whatever it took to take care of her mother's changing needs.

Who knows where Barb will find herself in her work situation, or in her circumstances with her mom. But isn't that life? And isn't it, dare I say, rather wonderful?

Your beliefs, your attitudes, and your experiences shape your life. And your life—the twists and turns along your path— in turn shapes your beliefs, your attitudes, and your experiences. It's a lovely dance, if you're willing to simply bend into it and go with the flow.

Most people rail against the uncertainty and changes of life. Not my friend and fellow thespian, Forry Buckingham, who is one of the most positive, enthusiastic people I have never met. "You know what's great about being an actor?" he once asked me. "You never know what's going to happen next!" Now *that's* a useful attitude.

FAITH, FLOW, AND TRUST

I don't know when I started to use the expression "it is what it is," but it's one of my pet sayings. When faced with something unexpected, I say it out loud, "it is what it is." And then I do my best to go with the flow. I tend to trust that all is as it should be, and all is being revealed to me. The more I trust that the next step will be revealed, or that there is a positive lesson or blessing to be gained from even the most awful situation, the less stress or anxiety I feel.

I recently watched a lovely Oscar-nominated documentary called *the Tsunami and the Cherry Blossom* by filmmaker Lucy Walker. It is, on one hand, a harrowing documentary about the gargantuan earthquake and ensuing tsunami that occurred in Japan in March 2011, wiping out entire families, towns, and villages. It is also, on the other hand, a testimony to the power of endurance, the power of faith, and the power of trust. As time passes, the cherry trees still standing among the ravaged landscape begin to bloom. And as the flowers unfurl and blossom, so, too, does the hope and the fate of tsunami victims who have lost everything. At the end of the movie, one young woman stands on a high hill, near a flowering cherry tree, surveying what remains of her home town—what appear to be miles of splintered houses, twisted cars, and other detritus. Smiling, she points out signs of renewal and regeneration—construction projects, areas that are slowly being cleaned and ordered. And then she shares her conviction that by the time the cherry trees bloom again in the year that follows, there will be even more progress—just as there will be the year after that.[II]

That is faith, flow, and trust in action.

Faith—trusting somehow, that there is an order to things, that all is meant to be, "it is what it is"—allows us to flow into each moment and take little steps or great leaps forward into the Wild Why Not. It's what allowed Sheryl, the medical doctor from chapter twelve, to turn her life on its ear and complete a career changing fellowship. As she put it, "I realized I was jumping into a complete unknown." Did that stop her? Not for a second.

LOOK FOR THE LEITMOTIF (UNDERLYING THEME)

In opera, the musical term leitmotif is used to describe a recurring short melodic phrase or theme used to suggest a specific character—think of the menacing musical theme "da DA da DA da DA" that's played every time the shark in the movie *Jaws* is within biting distance.

I like to think the underlying leitmotif of your unique purpose—or soul role—snakes through your life, announcing itself by shaking you alive when you are in its presence.

I often ask my clients to consider what their leitmotif might be. What is the theme of their lives, the unique, unifying purpose that has been present in anything of meaning they have ever done? What one archetypal word, like "artist," "healer," "mother," or "catalyst," can they use to define the essence of their leitmotif?

When I was working with a client I'll name Carol, we spent some time drilling down to what her soul role might be. Carol is an accomplished visual artist and designer, and the owner of a successful marketing and website development company. After much discussion, we determined that Carol's soul role is to bring creative projects to life. Then we brainstormed to find a single word that represents the theme of Carol's soul role. "I've got it," said Carol, "I'm a doula!" A doula, in case you don't know, is someone who helps women give birth. In Carol's case, Carol uses her gifts, the song in her (her creative abilities, insight, people skills) to, among other things, help people birth gorgeous websites from the snippet of an idea. She has most recently catalyzed a successful networking organization into being. Carol is a doula, whether or not she ever helps bring a real live baby into the world.

A coaching client and business owner I'll call Denise uplifts and expands everyone she touches with her joyful, boundless enthusiasm. When I asked her to come up with a word defining the leitmotif or recurring theme that threads through her life and work, Denise immediately chose "amplifier."

It's a perfect metaphor for the work she's currently doing—amplifying people's presence on the Internet so they can have more impact.

No matter what Carol or Denise choose to do in their lifetimes, no matter the form or expression, you can be sure that their lives will always have, at the core, the leitmotif that reflects their soul role.

Look back at the footsteps that, one after the other, have formed your path thus far. Notice the underlying pattern or theme that emerges. At the core of everything meaningful you've ever done throbs the heady music of your leitmotif, announcing and reaffirming the unique purpose you were born to express, using the unique gifts that are yours to share. Your leitmotif has been a consistent, insistent presence at every major shift, change, zig and zag in your life's path. Like a trusted, reliable friend, your leitmotif is there for you, always and forever, no matter what. The constant presence of your leitmotif is like a cosmic thumbs-up, reassuring you that wherever you are is exactly where you need to be. This realization can be of great comfort, especially when you are on the verge of making a brave leap from the safety of what you know into the heady unknown of the Wild Why Not.

Have faith that you are doing exactly what you should be doing in this very moment, even if it's not exactly as you expected it to be.

Flow into the opportunities that present themselves to you. Leap fearlessly into what needs to be done to honor and express your soul role.

And finally, trust that all is well, "it is what it is." You have the power, the insight, and the ability to *know what you need to know and do what you need to do*—in your life and your work.

SAY "AAA"

**On a separate piece of paper, answer the following questions
and complete the following exercises:**

ATTITUDE

• What is your general attitude about trust/leaping into the Wild Why
Not or having faith?

• What affirmation can you create, repeat, and embrace to maintain
a more positive attitude towards having faith/trusting whatever
comes next (e.g., "Because I believe that all is as it's meant to be,
I trust each moment as it unfolds.")?

ACTION

1. Imagine wearing glasses that allow you to clearly see the connections between the cosmic clues that have guided you step by step
on your life path. Where along that path did you choose to simply
surrender and trust that all would work out for the best?

2. How do you think your life or work might change for the better
if you were willing to trust more and fear less? If you were willing to
believe that everything was working out for your highest good?

3. If you could push fear of the unknown aside and simply leap
ahead, what action would you take that you are currently avoiding?

4. Think back to a time when you were happily surprised by the
difference between what you fearfully imagined might happen and
what actually happened (e.g., the reality of parachuting out of a plane
versus the idea or anticipation of doing it). What did you learn from
that experience?

5. What is the leitmotif that snakes through your life, your work? If you were to choose a single word that reflects the essence of your leitmotif (e.g. "teacher" or "motivator") what would it be?

6. What *one* action step are you willing to take this week to encourage yourself to trust more and fear the unknown less?

ACCOUNTABILITY
What will you do/what system of accountability will you put into place to help yourself complete this week's action step?

Coda

LEAVING A LEGACY

If I want, I can lead the way,
I can make a choice, I can claim this day.
If I want, I can lend a hand,
I can make a choice, and take a stand
and hope begins with me.

ELENI KELAKOS, "HOPE BEGINS WITH ME," *TOUCH THE SKY*

The audience *shifting, waiting.*
Backstage, I hold my guitar close to me, feeling, through its weathered wood, the
thump of my heart.
A woman in a sharp suit speaks into a microphone:

"Ladies and Gentlemen, the speaker you're about to meet has spent a lifetime
on stage. First, as a professional actress in New York and Los Angeles. Then, as
an award-winning, nationally touring singer and songwriter, with four CDs,
released on her own label, EEK! Records. Finally, as a professional speaker,
inspiring people like you to embrace their uniqueness and step into their power.

When she's not on the speaking platform, Eleni leads out as a coach and trainer, helping other people speak and lead with confidence, impact, and influence. She's on a mission to get people—and women in particular—to stop playing small so they can make the difference they were born to make.

And she's here to share tools and techniques to help you do exactly that. Please welcome Eleni!"

I hear the applause and feel three hundred pairs of eyes watching. The seams of the stage are underfoot. The lights warm my face.

I like this. I really like this.

Applause, like a big hug.

No, I don't like this. I love this.

I take three deep breaths and step up to the podium.

Home again.

As of this writing, it's been ten years since I moved to Ann Arbor, Michigan, to be with Jim. Ten years of near-constant change, of flux, of development.

I have buried my mother.

Married the love of my life.

Become an instant mom to three step-kids.

Gained three cats and lost two more.

Added more precious members to my choir.

And danged if I haven't become something I never dreamed I'd be—a professional speaker. I use stories, songs, and the practical theatre tools that shaped me to inspire people to embrace what I call their transformational presence—the ability to be so fully and authentically present, so fully in alignment with their soul role, that they deeply impact the way others feel, think, or behave.

When I am not speaking, I help others speak and present themselves more confidently and convincingly. I am, to say the least, nuttycrazythrilled about the work I do. Because when I look into the eyes and the souls of the men and women I work with, I recognize something familiar: A great longing to be who they really are, singing their unique song to the world. This longing collides with their inherent uncertainty. Should I? Could I? Can I risk being different? Can I risk showing and being who I really am? Do I dare do and be everything I can do and be? Especially if it's different or flies in the face of what other people believe or value?

Having spent my life wrestling with these questions, and chosen, at last, to accept myself and show up in the world as I really am, I feel uniquely qualified to help my clients. What's more, I feel a great desire to help them. It's what rockets me out of bed in the morning.

TOUCH THE SKY

My delivery methods have changed—and will probably continue to change—as I strive to move my message further and further out into the world. Reflecting my unique passions and gifts, I've gone from acting, to singing, writing, and recording songs; to creating and delivering workshops; to hanging up my shingle as a presentation coach and trainer; to firing up people's hearts and souls as a motivational speaker; to writing blogs, articles, a journal of motivational musings, and now, this book you hold in your hands. Each delivery method has been a link, forming a perfect chain, leading to where I am today.

But always, no matter its method of delivery, my core message—the slogan or leitmotif of my life—remains the same as the title of this book: "Touch the sky." After over fifty years on this planet, I can say, without discomfort or apology, that I am, indeed, a healer, just as the woman in Macy's told me I was when I was reaching out to passersby with fragrant lotion. I am also a way-shower, just as Richard Hatch, the workshop leader from the Celebrate Life retreat, insisted I was. I am a healer and a way-shower. If I could reduce it down to one word, I would say I am an elevator—my soul role is to elevate others, exhorting them to *stop playing small* so they can make the difference they were born to make.

When I think about it, I see that awareness of my soul role, of my desire to elevate others, has always been there—even in my darkest moments. Recently, I dusted off the contents of the "Yearly Goals" file I started in 1987. The seven words that led off the faded, lined pages of planning work I did with Gary back in New York leaped out at me, still powerful, still relevant: "Sang for the world. Was Happy. Gave." Delving deeper into the file, I found two statements from ensuing years that startled me: "To touch people the world over, on and offstage..." said the first, from 1988. "To use my gifts as a communicator with joy and passion to heal and illuminate," said the second, from 1990. There it is, in black and white: Evidence that more than twenty years ago, I was, even then, shaping my work in deference to the needs and nature of my soul role.

What's important is this: I've gone from living for the applause that comes from being on a stage, to living for the joy of applauding others as they reach for the best in them. I'm not saying I don't love receiving applause—once a diva, always a diva. But what really makes my toes curl, what really gives me the cosmic goosebumps, is changing the way people feel and think about themselves so they can take action and manifest their greatness. In order to do that, I have to model what I ask of them: I have to be willing to be authentic and in the moment. I have to be willing to be prepared and to reach for the best in me, choosing to touch the sky in the face of obstacles. I have to be willing to do whatever it takes to keep the flame of my transformational presence stoked and alive. I have to be willing to turn myself on and stay turned on, in spite of obstacles.

IGNITE YOUR TRANSFORMATIONAL PRESENCE

The five commandmentsof great acting, great speaking, and great leadership, which I've referred to, obliquely, throughout these pages, are Know Thyself; Be Thyself; Prepare Thyself; Commit Thyself; and Turn Thyself on, So You Can Turn Others On. Each is an essential building block of transformational presence. The last commandment, however, is key. Because *you*—turned on, fully present, fully alive, fully aligned with your soul role, fully embracing your unique gifts and talents—can change the world, one person, one word, one action at a time. When you're turned on, you turn other people on. When you're living a life that honors and expresses the song in you, applying your passions, talents, and gifts to your unique soul role, not only do you fulfill the unique role you are here to play on Planet Earth—you lead the way for others to do the same.

Your fully activated transformational presence has the power to change not only the course of your life, but other people's lives as well.

I cannot think of a better example than that of the poet I'll call John.

John was in the audience of a musical performance I gave at a local coffee-house three days after the fire that took my cat and my home. Raw, emotionally shattered, and unmoored, I did not hide myself from my audience. I stayed vulnerable and honest, sharing my deep sense of loss, pouring my feelings into my songs. There were many tears and a surprising amount of laughter. It was one of the toughest—and most satisfying—performances of my life. And the audience—a mix of supportive friends and strangers—was with me every step of the way.

The following morning, I awoke to find an email from John. We'd met in passing the night before. He'd given me a particularly heartfelt squeeze after the show, muttering "Thank you" into my ear with a peculiar vehemence. When I read his email, I understood why. He had been feeling hopeless, suicidal. In the darkest funk, he happened onto my show. When I started to sing and play, something shifted in him. My courage and willingness to defy the obstacles and show up in all my vulnerability that evening somehow made him think *If she can go on, so can I.*

John and I became dear friends and great supporters of each other's work. And I am forever grateful that I made the choice to show up on that stage that night. Who knows what might have become of John if I had not.

Think about it. Whose life might you affect for the better by your willingness to show up in each moment of your life, all cylinders blasting? You are deeply needed, whether you know it or not.

YOUR RESIDUAL EFFECT

Actors sometime use the term *residual effect* to refer to the lingering mood or feeling left behind by a fellow actor who has just left the stage. As a human being, you also leave behind a residual effect through the actions and the choices you make in the play that is your life. So, be mindful of the trail you leave behind. The attitude you exude and the actions you take throughout your life have the ability to affect others deeply and profoundly, for better or for worse, depending on your choice.

WHAT WILL YOU CHOOSE?

So.

What about you?

What turns you on? What gives you the cosmic goosebumps? And are you choosing to pay attention to them? Are you choosing to pay attention to what you love, what you're good at, and what you *know* is right for you?

And what about your soul role, the purpose that is uniquely yours? Are you choosing to honor it and to serve it using the song in you—the gifts, talents, dreams, and abilities with which you were blessed? Or are you choosing to hide in the basement, keeping yourself and the song in you small and sheltered?

Are you choosing to stoke the flame of your transformational presence, keeping your passion and your purpose alive so you can persevere when the no's pound like the blows of a hammer? Are you choosing to protect and nurture your passion and your purpose, remembering that "No one can take away your power, unless you let them"? Or are you choosing to be a parts car, giving away the best parts of yourself to others at the expense of your very dear, very worthy self?

Are you choosing to honor the triple A's, choosing a can-do attitude, taking consistent action and holding yourself accountable for those actions on a daily basis? Or are you choosing to slither away from the responsibility of actualizing your own life?

Are you choosing your choir wisely, surrounding yourself with helpers, people who lift you up with their love and support? Or are you choosing to spend your precious time with hoovers, people intent on dragging you down into the soul-sucking muck of Bittertown?

Are you choosing to have the courage to show yourself to the world as you really are, in all your flawed magnificence—at home, at work, in your words, and in your actions? Or are you choosing to shrink to fit, denying the very things that make you uniquely you?

And in the face of obstacles—and there are, and will forever be, obstacles— are you choosing to see them as the gift they are, as the opportunity to ask yourself the all-important questions, "Will I choose to play small, or will I choose to touch the sky?"

The choice is yours.

There is always a choice.

So choose wisely.

Define, embrace, and share your voice

Speak, live, and lead with authenticity.

Make the difference you were born to make.

Because you matter.

Who you are matters.

And I believe in you.

References

[1]Ferdinand Foch. As quoted in *The 32d Infantry Division in World War II* (1956) by Harold Whittle Blakeley, p. 3

[2]Unknown

[3]Spoken by the actor Steve Carell (playing Barry Speck) in the movie *Dinner for Schmucks*, Paramount Pictures, 2010

[4]Anna Fels, "Do Women Lack Ambition?" *Harvard Business Review*, April, 2004.

[5]Dr Bruce Lipton, "The Honeymoon Effect," lecture presented at I can Do It! Conference, Toronto, May 15, 2011

[6]Marianne Williamson, *A Return to Love, (New York: Harper Collin, 1994)* p.107

[7]http://thinkexist.com/quotation/without_leaps_of_imagination-or_dreaming-we_lose/13520.htmlGloria Steinem quote Thinkexist.com, August 8, 2012

[8]Ibid

[9]Jihad Sadat, *a Woman of Egypt* (New York: Simon & Schuster 1987), p. 285

[10]Noah Baumbach (Director), & Scott Rudin (Producer). (2012) *Greenberg*. United States: Focus Features

[11]Lucy Walker (Director) (2011) *the Tsunami and the Cherry Blossom*. United States: Supply and In Demand Integrated

Acknowledgements

Let's call this what it is—a love letter to the members of my personal and professional choir who have loved me, informed me, shaped me, trusted me, encouraged me, and otherwise made my voice stronger, better, and wiser over many years. The book you hold is a reflection of their precious presence in my life. I am grateful beyond measure to walk—or have walked—beside them.

To anyone who has graced my path, even for a moment, and taught me, moved me, or reminded me about an essential piece of myself, thank you. You provided me with cosmic clues that have shaped my life.

To the core choir members whose enthusiasm, frankness, and unconditional support have lifted me to my level best and whose character and insight have informed this book: Amy Albert, Brigitte Lehnert, Suzi Winson, Chris Wucherer, Carrie Hensel, Betsy Volaric, Sherene McHenry, Virginia Giordano, Forry and Beth Buckingham, Lorel Vidlund, Kathy Eubanks, Marilyn Suttle, Connie Kaldor, Thor Edgell, and the irrepressible Doug Messenger. You are each a precious gift to me. Thank you for listening and for egging me on.

The deepest gratitude to Dr. Jeffrey Laham for truly seeing me and helping me see—and save—myself. You changed my life. Thank you, Sanda Jasper, for forever altering the way I think and believe. I am humbled and grateful for your loving wisdom, guidance, and friendship. Richard Hatch, fellow way-shower, I will always be grateful to you for gently pushing me to step onto the stage and share my wisdom. Thank you, Louise Hay—your words, your voice, your wisdom pulled me from the edge.

A heartfelt bow to the teachers who saw and encouraged the best in me: Irving Bloom, for making ninth grade English class a wonder, informing me that I had writing in my bones and assuring me that rules were sometimes meant to be broken; Steven Byk, for telling me I could be a professional actress and meaning it; Sigmund Sobel—now adding your wattage to heaven—for showing me that teaching others could be loving and fun; Dick Rousseau for celebrating and nurturing my acting talent; Mr. Rich, for showcasing and encouraging my songwriting; Richard Lavache, for allowing me to go to the music room and plink on the piano instead of daydreaming in study hall; Raymond Thompson, for teaching me how to think; Jim Barnhill for always believing in me and insisting I major in theatre arts when I wasn't so sure; Don Wilmeth, for casting me anyway; Warren Robertson, for giving me permission to just be myself; Michael Howard, for giving me the tools to be myself under pressure, and maintaining a loving creative space that nurtured me during challenging times.

And then there are the professional choir members whose guidance or expertise has helped to make my vision a reality: Anne Bogart, thank you for always challenging me ("could be more!") to bring my creative best to every rehearsal or performance. Carol Reynolds, thank you for seeing something in me I couldn't yet see myself. Gary Hibbard, immense gratitude for teaching me to run my business like a donut shop. Fred Gorman—gone, but not forgotten these many years—I will always be grateful for your willingness to stand by me when others would not and, in 1984, for suggesting I write a book (OK, so it took a while). Marty Somberg, of Somberg Design, thank you for the understated elegance of your design work and for always getting it right. Sharron Stockhausen, I so appreciate your painstaking editorial work, generosity of spirit and sense of humor. Mike Hensel, of In Motion Studios, many thanks for helping me shape and share my voice through your video production. Carrie Hensel, Catherine Hayes, Alaine Karoleff, and everyone at Inner Circle Media: Thank you for always turning yourself inside out to make my message sing and reach the folks who need it. C and C, you are both like family to me, and I adore you. Mark Le Blanc, coach, mentor, beloved friend—what a blessing to have you in my corner. Thank you for honoring me by writing a foreword and for keeping this book moving ahead to completion.

Many thanks to Sheryl Kurze, Lauren Parrott, Emily Hay, Shelley Fitzgerald, Sandra Carter, Steve Fischbein, Joanne Grosh, Kevin Gillespie, Delfina Bonilla-Cassel, and Miche Suboski for letting me share your stories and your wisdom. And a huge, loving thanks to all of my Blue Sky Coaching and public speaking coaching and training clients whose stories and experiences informed the teachings of this book. If you see yourself, obliquely, in the preceding pages, I thank you, and I hope I have honored you. For every lesson I have taught you, you have taught me two.

Thanks, also, to Jana Stanfield, for helping me see that combining music and speaking could not just be possible or profitable, but deeply meaningful. I so appreciate your generosity and for introducing me to the wonderful world of the National Speakers Association.

And then there is the loving and supportive family I am blessed to have married into during the second half of my life: Dottie and Mark Fleming, (a.k.a. Mama II and Dad II); sis-in-law, Cathy/Katy (your strong voice as a woman and mother is an inspiration); step-kids J.C., Elliot, and Kira; niece Sarah; granddaughter and grandson Sarah and Luka. To the young ones making their way in the world I say, "Be you, aim high." I love you each to pieces.

It seems impossible that two of my biggest influences are not here to thank and hug: My mother, Theresa Plakias Kelakos, who helped me see the world through the eyes of a playful and passionate artist, and my father, Michael George Kelakos, who taught me that there is much more to see than what our eyes reveal. My greatest teachers, we converse regularly in my dreams.

Bro George, thank you for lending me your guitar, teaching me how to play it, and using your silver tongue to persuade Ma and Daddy to buy me a guitar of my own. Your musicianship and your passion for life are an inspiration, and I love you.

Deep gratitude to the folks who have cast me, booked me, and otherwise stepped up to help me ply my trade on the airwaves and on stages large and small. A collective hug to my colleagues, the musicians, speakers, authors, and coaches who change people's lives one song or one word at a time: Thanks for your continued inspiration. To the audiences who have drunk in my music and my words, beamed back your love and laughter, and shared your stirring stories with me, I especially thank you. You are why I do what I do.

Finally—and always—my beloved husband, Jim. Three times really is a charm. You never fail to believe in me, even when I turn into Medea. Thank you for tolerating the hours spent away from you, on weekends and late into the night, hammering away at this book. Every day with you is a gift.

About Eleni Kelakos

Eleni is the founder and CTO (Chief Transformational Officer) of The Eleni Group, a coaching and training company in Ann Arbor, Michigan. As a professional actress, nationally touring singer-songwriter and recording artist with four acclaimed music CDs, Eleni spent over twenty years learning how to bring her most authentic and effective self to interviews, auditions, and performances on countless stages from New York to Hollywood. She shares those tools with business professionals who want to feel more confident, impactful, and influential in their speeches, presentations, life and leadership.

Eleni presents motivational keynote programs (*Touch the Sky; Stop Playing Small; and Think Like an Actor, Speak Like a Pro*), that combine original songs, stories, and actionable content to professional groups and associations across the country. She's particularly zealous about working with and speaking to women, encouraging them to stop playing small in their lives and work and to use their words, body language, and actions to convey confident leadership.

A graduate of Brown University, Eleni is a past president of the National Speakers Association of Michigan. She shares a happy, fur-covered home with her husband, Jim Fleming, and their three cats, Zeke, Tippy, and Cicely (who, in their own way, each had a paw in writing this book).

Interested in having Eleni speak at your next event, facilitate a training program for your company, or work with you as a coach? Write to booking@theelenigroup.com.

To watch videos of Eleni, read her blog, visit her store, or find out more about her services and products, visit: www.theelenigroup.com.

Join the conversation! Like *The Eleni Group* on Facebook, and follow Eleni Kelakos on Twitter.

Also by Eleni Kelakos

30 Days and 30 Ways to Touch the Sky! A Journal

Music CDs:
Touch the Sky: (Volume One) Songs to Inspire, Uplift and Empower
Where I Come From
To the Bone
I Will Fly

Available for purchase at **www.theelenigroup.com/store**
For bulk orders, call **734-622-0522**
or write to **booking@theelenigroup.com**